A Guide to
Effective
Resource
Development

Advancing Christian Higher Education

Wesley K. Willmer
Editor

 Coalition for Christian Colleges
& Universities

As a professional association of academic institutions, the Coalition for Christian Colleges & Universities focuses on helping Christian colleges and universities better fulfill their mission to effectively integrate scholarship, faith, and service. The Coalition coordinates professional development opportunities for administrators and faculty, off-campus student programs, public advocacy for Christ-centered higher education, and cooperative efforts among member colleges and universities.

Founded in 1976 and incorporated in 1982, the Coalition has a membership of 90 four-year colleges and universities. Member institutions are the focus and core of the Coalition, but the association also involves a growing number of affiliated institutions of higher education in the United States and around the world.

The Coalition is a member of the Evangelical Council for Financial Accountability, the National Association of Independent Colleges and Universities, and the Christian Stewardship Association. The Coalition also holds associate membership in the Council of Independent Colleges.

Through the years, numerous foundations, businesses, and individuals have supported the Coalition and its programs, in addition to dues from member institutions and fees for various programs. The Coalition is a nonprofit, tax exempt organization under section 501(c)(3) of the IRS code. For additional information, please contact the Coalition for Christian Colleges & Universities at 329 Eighth Street NE, Washington, DC 20002-6158.

Telephone: (202) 546-8713
Fax: (202) 546-8913
E-mail: Coalition@cccu.org

ISBN 0-9652730-1-6

Table of Contents

Tables and Figures   v

Foreword   vii

Preface   ix

Acknowledgments   xii

Chapter 1 Christian Higher Education Advancement in Overview   1
Wesley K. Willmer

Chapter 2 Presidents: Effective Fundraising Leadership   19
G. Blair Dowden

Chapter 3 Development through the Eyes of Faith   53
Adam J. Morris

Chapter 4 The Alumni Connection   73
Jeffrey J. Krimmel

Chapter 5 Eight Critical Topics in Enrollment Management   89
Peter Harkema and Dale Kuiper

Chapter 6 Public Relations in Advancement: Targeting for Results   117
John L. Glancy

Chapter 7 Trustees: Their Essential Leadership Function   145
Robert C. Andringa

Appendices   160

    A: CCCU Membership Map

    B: Resource Development Survey

    C: Responding Institutions

Tables and Figures

Table 1-1	Institution Size by Undergraduate Enrollment (FTE)	3
Table 1-2	Institution Size by Graduate Enrollment (FTE)	3
Table 1-3	Age of Responding Institutions	4
Table 1-4	Denominational Affiliation	5
Table 1-5	Total Educational and General (E&G) Expenditures	5
Table 1-6	Endowment Size	6
Figure 1-1	Average Dollar Endowment by Group Size in Three Time Periods (in millions)	6
Table 1-7	Total Mailing List by Enrollment Size	7
Table 1-8	Alumni Mailing List by Enrollment Size	7
Table 1-9	Mailing List, Excluding Alumni, by Enrollment Size	8
Table 1-10	Percentage of Those on Mailing List Who Gave at Least One Gift Per Year	8
Table 1-11	Number of Mailings	9
Table 1-12	Funding the Budget: Percent of Education Budget Met by Size	10
Figure 1-2	Funding the Budget	11
Table 1-13	Advancement Expenditures by Enrollment Size	11
Table 1-14	Percentage of Educational and General (E&G) Expenditures Allocated to Advancement by Enrollment Size	12
Figure 1-3	1994 Resource Development Expenditures by Enrollment Size	12
Table 1-15	Number of Advancement Professionals (FTE) by Institutional Enrollment Size	13
Table 1-16	Number of Clerical/Secretarial Personnel in Advancement (FTE) by Institutional Enrollment Size	14
Figure 1-4	Use of Consultants	15
Figure 2-1	Presidential Time Allocation	26
Figure 2-2	Allocation of President's Time to Advancement Functions	26
Figure 2-3	Smith's Five I's of Fundraising	31
Table 2-1	Qualifications for Hiring a Chief Development Officer	35
Figure 2-4	Presidential Contacts—May	38
Figure 2-5	Position Prior to Assuming Presidency	41
Figure 2-6	Previous Presidential Positions	41
Figure 2-7	How Presidents Learn Fundraising	42
Table 3-1	Fundraising Expenditures: (Including Salaries and Benefits, Travel, Media/Promotion, etc.) by Enrollment Size	56
Table 3-2	Fundraising Expenditures: Percentage of Total Development Expenditures by Enrollment Size	57

Table 3-3	Cost to Raise $1 (Fundraising Expenditures Divided by Total Capital + Operations + Endowment)	58
Table 3-4	Professional Fundraising Staff (FTE) by Enrollment Size	59
Table 3-5	Fundraising Clerical/Secretarial Staffing (FTE) by Institutional Enrollment Size	60
Table 3-6	Position Prior to Becoming Chief Development Officer	61
Table 3-7	Time CDOs Spend on Major Prospects	62
Table 3-8	Areas in which CDOs, Staff Need Additional Training (%)	62
Table 3-9	CDOs' Assessment of Change in Dollar Goals (%) 1989	64
Table 3-10	Operations Gifts Received by Enrollment Size	65
Table 3-11	Capital Gifts Received by Enrollment Size	66
Table 3-12	Endowment Gifts Received by Enrollment Size	67
Table 3-13	Gift Sources by Constituent Group (Excluding Tuition)	68
Table 3-14	Generators of Income (%) 1989	68
Table 4-1	Alumni Office Professionals (FTE) by Enrollment Size	74
Table 4-2	Alumni Office Expenditures by Enrollment Size	75
Figure 4-1	The Committed Alumni Decision Process	78
Table 4-3	Alumni Office Expenditures: Percent of Total Resource Development Expenditures by Enrollment	86
Table 4-4	Alumni Office Clerical/Secretarial Staffing (FTE) by Enrollment	86
Table 5-1	Admissions Expenditures (Including Salaries and Benefits, Travel, Media/Promotion, etc.) by Enrollment Size	95
Table 5-2	Admissions Recruitment Expenditures: Percentage of Total Resource Development Expenditures by Enrollment Size	95
Table 5-3	Recruiting/Admissions Professionals (FTE) by Enrollment Size	96
Table 5-4	Recruiting/Admissions Clerical/Secretarial Staff (FTE) by Enrollment Size	96
Figure 5-1	Female College Continuation Rates 1960 to 1993	100
Table 6-1	Public Relations Goals of Institution (frequency count)	122
Table 6-2	Institutional Image (frequency count)	126
Table 6-3	Public Relations Expenditures by Enrollment Size	127
Table 6-4	Public Relations Expenditures: Percentage of Total Resource Development Expenditures by Enrollment Size	128
Table 6-5	Public Relations Professional Personnel (FTE) by Enrollment Size	128
Table 6-6	Public Relations Clerical/Secretarial Staffing (FTE) by Enrollment Size	129
Table 7-1	Important Characteristics When Recruiting New Trustees	151
Table 7-2	Trustee Giving Ability	154
Table 7-3	Why Trustees Limit Their Involvement in Fundraising	154
Table 7-4	Ranking of Trustee Effectiveness	156
Table 7-5	Trustee Satisfaction in Advancement-related Activities	156

Foreword

Since the founding of Harvard in 1636, private colleges have been learning how better to "advance" their institutions. The task seems to become more critical with each passing decade.

All of private higher education faces new challenges requiring new friends and new strategies. In 1995, private four-year colleges enrolled about 3 million out of 15 million enrolled in American higher education. Projections to the year 2005 by the U.S. Department of Education show only 3.2 million students in these institutions, holding the same 20 percent of the total. Within this big universe, 90 Coalition schools enroll about 150,000 future leaders in the body of Christ.

There have been periods in our history when the "experts" predicted the days of small liberal arts colleges were numbered. Amazingly, more have survived than most would predict. But many—including church-related colleges—have also closed their doors. As Proverb 27:23-4 reminds us, "Be sure you know the condition of your flocks, give careful attention to your herds; for riches do not endure forever, and a crown is not secure for all generations."

We believe God has His hand on Christian higher education. It is where followers of Christ learn to love Him with all their minds. A Christian worldview gives students a framework for continued learning. Relationships are made that last a lifetime. Undergraduate teaching is still the focus on our campuses. People are valued and nurtured in close community. Yet, to stand still in today's world is to slip behind. Depending on God for wisdom, we who care about and have been given leadership responsibility for these institutions must learn and apply the God-honoring principles found in these pages.

My desire is that this book will encourage, affirm, and teach campus leaders and friends to build even stronger institutions. Never has the need for Christ-centered education been greater in our society. We are indebted to the consistent leadership of Dr. Wes Willmer, vice president at Biola University, one of our member institutions, for coordinating this book and its predecessor, **Friends, Funds, and Freshmen** (1990). His vision led to a three-year Lilly grant so ably directed by Dr. Rebekah Basinger, now vice president for development at Houghton College, another Coalition member.

As you learn from the gifted authors of the chapters that follow, please pray for those others who will read and lead these special institutions.

Robert C. Andringa, president
Coalition for Christian Colleges & Universities
Washington, DC

Preface

It is a well established fact that American higher education is immersed in a difficult era—increased competition, high costs, funding cut backs, and eroding public confidence are but some of the gnawing issues. Those institutions identifying themselves as Christian colleges and universities are not immune from these broader issues and have an additional set of concerns and pressures as their faith commitments collide with a secularizing culture.

A key component to the future viability of higher education is the ability to attract students, raise funds, and sustain friendships that support the mission of the institution. The purpose of this book is to focus on those unique concerns of advancing Christian higher education and not to duplicate existing literature in the field.

The Coalition for Christian Colleges & Universities (CCCU) has a book series entitled "Through The Eyes of Faith" which looks at various disciplines from a Christian perspective. Following this concept, this publication is an attempt to provide a guide to Christian higher education advancement activities from a biblical world view which recognizes that all resources are God-given, and we are called to be faithful stewards of our time, talents, and treasures. The intent is to provide a practical resource guide for presidents, trustees, staff, volunteers, consultants, and others working to promote goodwill and support among these institutions.

The initiative for this effort comes from Lilly Endowment, Inc. funding which provided for a 1989 study which was published in the book, **Friends, Funds, and Freshmen**, and a 1994 follow-up study at the culmination of a three-year grant program focusing on fundraising effectiveness. A preceding study concluded in 1984 (Willmer) is referred to occasionally. The 1994 survey was mailed to the 89 member institutions of the Coalition for Christian Colleges & Universities. Seventy-five institutions responded.

My desire is that this book be a helpful and encouraging resource to those working hard to advance Christian higher education.

Wesley K. Willmer
Biola University
La Mirada, California

Acknowledgments

A team effort made this book possible. Many people from across the country gave sacrificially to assure this project's completion. It was a growing and learning experience and one in which each of us involved in the project can look back and say it was worth the effort if it helps our colleagues.

A special word of thanks goes to the Lilly Endowment, Inc. which provided the funding for the project. Of special recognition is Charles A. Johnson, retired vice president for development at the endowment, and Fred L. Hofheinz, program director in the religion division, for their helpfulness and involvement in facilitating the project.

The publishing of this book resulted from the prompting of Karen Longman, Coalition for Christian Colleges & Universities (CCCU) vice president, the encouragement of Bob Andringa, CCCU president, and Rebekah B. Basinger, vice president for development at Houghton College who coordinated the 1994 survey as one of her last duties as the project director for the three-year fundraising effectiveness project.

Jane Halteman (Wheaton, IL) played a significant role in the data collection, editing, production, and coordination of the project. Wheaton College Director of Publications, Georgia Douglass, provided the cover design, and Adam Morris of Biola University served as publication coordinator in working with the logistics of keeping the project moving.

Blair Dowden, presidential chapter author, wishes to acknowledge his colleagues at Huntington College who assisted him: Linda Taylor, administrative secretary to the president; Beth Lahr, administrative assistant to the president; John Paff, director of public relations; Robert E. Kaehr, director of library services, and Patricia A. Jones, assistant in library services.

As general editor, I wish to acknowledge the efforts of each chapter author and the assistance of Biola University employees Jan Araujo, Karen Denny, and Joan Wilson. I also wish to acknowledge my wife, Sharon, and children, Kristell, Stephen, and Brian. I also appreciate the friendship and encouragement of Clyde Cook, Biola University president.

Wesley K. Willmer, editor

Chapter 1

Christian Higher Education Advancement in Overview

WESLEY K. WILLMER

> "Without reliable, well-tested principles, we have nothing by which to judge the advice we receive or to give direction for our plans and actions." (Hobbs and Francis, 1974, p. 53)

One of the main reasons to put the time and effort into this publication is to provide written data for useful comparison and guidelines which help identify strengths and untapped potential of advancement functions in Christian colleges and universities. This publication provides a framework for managers to assess their operation in relationship to others and to compare their efforts in relationship to similar institutions over a several-year period. The intent is to provide standards that go beyond "knee-jerk thinking" (Willmer, 1984, page 72) in which we do the popular thing or whatever the pressure of the moment demands.

This book provides information about the Coalition for Christian Colleges & Universities (CCCU) member institutions and their advancement activities. This chapter more specifically describes the characteristic elements of the Christian college advancement function by giving descriptive data of the survey population to enhance understanding and comparison, both among the respondents to the current questionnaire (1994) as well as two previous studies conducted in 1984 and 1989 (**Friends, Funds and Freshmen**). This chapter provides an overview for the greater analysis portrayed in the remaining chapters and sets the stage for looking at advancement through the eyes of faith.

In comparing the three surveys (1984, 1989, and 1994) covering a 10-year span, 10 overview observations surface:

1. Graduate enrollment growth is modest and overall student population growth is most noticeable from newly-implemented degree completion programs.

2. There are no newly-founded institutions, and as expected, the existing ones are getting older. At least one college closed, and a couple merged to avoid closure. Membership in the CCCU continues to grow.

1

3. Endowment size grew with inflation—the big got bigger and the smaller endowments remained stable or had modest growth.

4. Mailing lists grew somewhat, as would be expected (along graduation growth lines), but not dramatically.

5. Average mailing frequencies of 4 newsletters (or principal publications) and 3.3 appeal letters per year remained essentially constant.

6. Tuition continues to cover an increasingly higher percentage of an institution's budget (72 vs. 66 percent over a five-year period).

7. Gift income is providing for a decreasing amount of the total institutional budget, down to 12 percent from 17 percent.

8. Income from other sources (auxiliary services, etc.) remained constant at 14 percent.

9. Total personnel in the overall advancement functions grew only slightly.

10. Total advancement budgets have grown slightly.

My sense is that institutional change is relatively minimal compared to the cultural/societal shifts that are changing around the institutions, and it seems helpful to look back and see where we have come from to have a better idea of where we are going.

Advancing Christian higher education requires managers to do a lot with a little. This generally means doing a few things well and not being everything to everyone. The greatest temptation is to try to duplicate the efforts of larger, more sophisticated (even among the Coalition) institutions. For applicability to individual institutions, the CCCU member institutions participating in the current survey are characterized, with the use of tables and graphs, generally by enrollment sizes.

Enrollment

Size of enrollment often correlates with budget size and gift income needs, so the size of the institutions in this study is used where possible. Colleges in the 751-1000 full-time equivalent (FTE) undergraduate enrollment category represent the largest segment (21 percent) of respondents to this study (see Table 1-1). In the 1985 study, the largest segment of respondents represented the up to 500 FTE undergraduate enrollment category (25 percent), and in 1989 the 501-750 (FTE) category was the largest (24 percent). This gradual growth demonstrates the continued strengthening of the small institutions. About half (51 percent) have enrollments of 1000 or less FTE undergraduates, 25 percent have 1001-1500 FTE undergraduate students, and 24 percent have more than 1501 students. In terms of comparing the data over the last five years, a dramatic shift occurred when several large institutions moved from the 1501-2000 category to the 2001+ enrollment size.

Table 1-1
Institution Size by Undergraduate Enrollment (FTE)

	# of Respondents			Relative Frequency (%)			Cumulative Frequency (%)		
Enrollment	1994	1989	1985	1994	1989	1985	1994	1989	1985
Up to 500	9	11	17	12	15	25	12	15	25
501-750	13	18	13	17	24	19	29	39	44
751-1000	16	13	13	21	18	19	50	57	63
1001-1250	11	12	7	15	16	10	65	73	73
1251-1500	8	5	7	11	7	10	76	80	83
1501-2000	7	8	8	9	11	12	85	91	95
2001+	11	7	3	15	9	5	100	100	100
Total	75	74	68	100	100	100			

Sixty-five schools (85 percent) which responded to the Resource Development Survey mailed to Coalition for Christian Colleges & Universities members in 1989, participated again in the 1994 survey. Of the 10 schools who participated in the 1994 survey but not in 1989, three responded to the first survey, and the other seven joined the CCCU after the second study.

Forty-one of the institutions (55 percent) who responded to the survey also offer graduate programs. Table 1-2 reveals the broad diversity in graduate enrollment with highs, lows, and means identified for each enrollment size category. The mean on the last line of the table (198) indicates the average enrollment of all 41 institutions with graduate enrollments rather than the average of the means for each enrollment category. When a bottom-line mean appears throughout this book, it reflects an average obtained by totaling the responses of all participants, not by totaling the means of each category.

Table 1-2
Institution Size by Graduate Enrollment (FTE)

	# Respondents		Highest		Lowest		Mean	
Enrollment	1994	1989	1994	1989	1994	1989	1994	1989
Up to 500	2	1	100	13	50	13	75	13
501-750	5	5	617	490	28	12	182	194
751-1000	10	5	1094	642	14	27	188	174
1001-1250	5	5	262	145	9	11	50	87
1251-1500	5	2	176	166	47	9	87	131
1501-2000	4	4	200	874	53	200	442	134
2001+	10	6	1021	776	41	25	249	453
Total	41	28			Survey Mean		198	220

Location

CCCU members are located throughout the United States, with some in Canada. (See Appendix A.) Thirty (41 percent) of the 75 respondents are located in the northern midwest of the United States, and the second largest concentration is the southeast, represented by 11 schools (15 percent). The remaining distribution is: 10 (13 percent) in the northeast; 9 (12 percent) in the southwest; 6 (8 percent) in the northwest; 6 (8 percent) in the southern midwest; and 3 (4 percent) in Canada.

Years in Existence

The 1994 survey (see Table 1-3) closely parallels the 1989 and 1985 surveys (as would be expected) with respect to the age of responding institutions. Seventy-one percent of those participating in 1994 are 51 years old or more, and 35 percent are more than 100 years old (25 percent in 1989). Several had centennial celebrations! Four percent are 25 years or younger (10 percent in 1989). The relatively long existence of these institutions is a good sign of health, because it provides a foundation of goodwill among an established base of alumni and friends.

Table 1-3
Age of Responding Institutions

Years of Existence	Number Responding		Percent	
	1994	1989	1994	1989
Less than 10 years	0	2	0	3
11-25 years	3	5	4	7
26-50 years	15	14	20	19
51-75 years	12	12	16	16
76-100 years	19	22	25	30
More than 100 years	26	19	35	25

Denominational Affiliations

As in the 1989 study, Baptist institutions in the 1994 study represented the largest denominational group (10 percent). See Table 1-4. The next largest groups were Nazarene and Presbyterian colleges at 7 percent each. (In the 1985 and 1989 study Nazarene and Presbyterian schools also were the second and third largest denominational groups represented in the study.) Eighteen percent of the respondents listed themselves as nondenominational. Both the control and support among these affiliations differed widely and can have a significant impact on the advancement function as it relates to board membership and gift income support.

Table 1-4
Denominational Affiliation

Denomination	1994 %	1989%	Denomination	1994%	1989%
Baptist	10	12	Brethren	3	4
Nazarene	7	9	Assemblies of God	3	3
Presbyterian	7	9	Christian Reformed	2	3
Mennonite	6	7	Friends	2	3
Church of God	1	5	Other	8	11
Free Methodist	4	5	Nondenominational	18	23
Wesleyan	4	5			

Expenditures

Table 1-5 breaks down educational and general (E&G) expenditures by indicating highs, lows, and means in the seven enrollment categories. Expenditures range from a low of $2,848,079 to a high of $41,058,042, and the mean for the entire sample is $9,469,952. At different points throughout the study a percentage of expenditures relative to these total E&G figures is used as a measure of resources allocated compared to the entire institutional budget.

Table 1-5
Total Educational and General (E&G) Expenditures

Enrollment	1994 High	1989 High	1994 Low	1989 Low	1994 Mean	1989 Mean
Up to 500	$6,003,162	$5,833,211	$2,848,079	$1,600,000	$4,633,257	$3,619,812
501-750	8,629,199	7,500,000	3,506,361	3,805,475	6,516,461	5,707,118
751-1000	13,256,984	13,507,584	5,600,000	4,096,359	9,846,965	7,824,707
1001-1250	17,200,085	14,084,000	8,001,330	4,750,933	13,314,058	8,999,338
1251-1500	19,000,000	15,764,766	10,696,943	8,601,635	14,423,532	11,985,487
1501-2000	24,695,823	25,300,000	10,854,307	8,887,043	17,159,242	17,681,459
2001+	41,058,042	30,672,000	13,834,987	12,100,000	29,531,791	22,125,563
Survey Mean of All Groups					$13,632,186	$9,469,952

Endowments

The range in endowment sizes at the member institutions is enormous—from zero to $120,000,000. The overall mean is $9,746,149 as evidenced in Table 1-6. The responding school's institutional endowments are graphed in Figure 1-1 by the number of colleges and amounts of their endowments (in millions of dollars). Responses from the 1985 and 1989 studies appear beside the current study data for comparison. As would be expected, endowments grew overall. Relatively speaking, the rich got richer, however, because of the leverage to make greater gains.

As a whole, Coalition for Christian Colleges & Universities colleges have very modest endowments. Only 21 institutions, or 28 percent, have endowments greater than $10 million. Six are under $1 million and 58 are between $1 million and $10 million. Remember that movement into different enrollment size groups accounts for many of the differences between study years.

Table 1-6
Endowment Size

Enrollment	1994 High	1989 High	1994 Low	1989 Low	1994 Mean	1989 Mean
Up to 500	$4,576,920	$7,000,000	$0	$0	$1,993,425	$1,719,850
501-750	21,000,000	16,500,000	29,660	182,473	5,992,279	3,299,324
751-1000	27,945,661	17,159,987	1,236,519	600,000	6,666,078	4,156,203
1001-1250	17,715,255	18,769,035	58,000	400,000	6,893,406	6,974,012
1251-1500	40,000,000	9,000,000	2,814,808	400,000	12,520,270	5,212,346
1501-2000	25,242,696	25,537,988	761,977	2,000,000	7,965,680	7,479,268
2001+	120,000,000	83,000,000	1,300,000	3,000,000	27,776,837	26,166,689
Survey Mean of All Groups					$9,746,149	$6,555,239

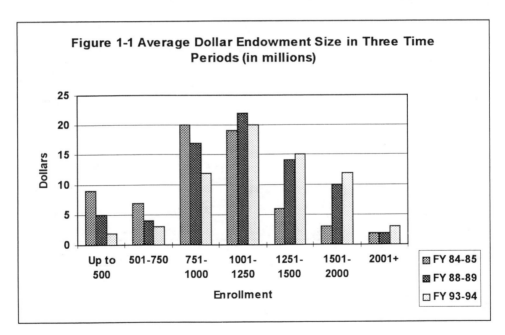

Figure 1-1 Average Dollar Endowment Size in Three Time Periods (in millions)

Mailing List Size

Generally, the size of an institution's mailing list gives an indication of the constituency size and provides the backbone for advancement communication activities. Among the CCCU colleges the lists of names ranged from a low of 2,000 to a high of 98,055. Table 1-7 displays the total mailing list (alumni and non alumni). Breakdowns between alumni and non alumni are shown in Tables 1-8 and 1-9.

Table 1-7
Total Mailing List by Enrollment Size

Enrollment	1994 High	1989 High	1994 Low	1989 Low	1994 Mean	1989 Mean
Up to 500	25,000	28,500	6,200	3,300	12,367	13,364
501-750	30,000	26,500	6,000	2,800	14,779	11,527
751-1000	37,000	26,000	2,000	6,487	14,550	15,102
1001-1250	79,100	70,000	4,000	5,300	22,365	21,082
1251-1500	20,000	20,000	4,000	10,100	15,000	16,125
1501-2000	96,214	61,000	9,544	10,500	32,709	29,678
2001+	98,055	70,000	11,602	12,500	34,250	30,481
Survey Mean of All Groups					19,971	17,777

Alumni mailing list sizes (Table 1-8) vary from a high of 25,000 names to a low of 700. As can be seen from the different means for the enrollment sizes, the lists generally get larger as enrollment increases.

Table 1-8
Alumni Mailing List by Enrollment Size

Enrollment	1994 High	1989 High	1994 Low	1989 Low	1994 Mean	1989 Mean
Up to 500	6,700	13,500	700	400	4,056	5,256
501-750	7,300	14,000	2,000	1,500	6,460	4,572
751-1000	13,000	13,318	700	3,200	7,111	7,406
1001-1250	17,000	14,693	2,500	1,800	7,985	9,384
1251-1500	12,500	18,000	3,000	6,000	9,835	9,310
1501-2000	28,000	16,488	5,000	10,000	8,950	16,400
2001+	25,085	30,000	9,000	7,000	15,826	15,713
Survey Mean of All Groups					8,550	8,716

There is not as much correlation between the sizes of the non alumni mailing lists and the sizes of the college enrollments. The sizes of mailing lists excluding alumni (see Table 1-9) vary from a low of 1,000 to a high of 84,000. The overall mean for the responding CCCU institutions is 11,582 non alumni names.

Table 1-9

Mailing List, Excluding Alumni, by Enrollment Size

Enrollment	1994 High	1989 High	1994 Low	1989 Low	1994 Mean	1989 Mean
Up to 500	22,000	20,000	1,600	3,000	8,311	9,522
501-750	16,000	29,000	2,500	1,666	9,037	7,968
751-1000	31,000	22,000	1,000	1,226	7,438	7,697
1001-1250	71,000	59,900	1,000	1,796	14,380	11,696
1251-1500	10,000	12,000	1,000	4,100	5,165	6,814
1501-2000	79,726	33,000	2,824	500	23,758	13,338
2001+	84,000	45,000	3,000	4,000	18,849	14,929
Survey Mean of All Groups					11,582	9,739

The effectiveness of soliciting to mailing lists is an important consideration for communication efforts. The survey asked, "What was the total percentage of those on your mailing list who gave at least one gift in FY 1993-94?" Table 1-10 shows the overall responses. Eighty-five percent said that 50 percent or less of their mailing lists contributed at least one gift. This probably means that 50 percent (or more) of the names are nondonors, and therefore the question must be asked, "What does it cost an institution to maintain names and process mailings to those who are probably nondonors?" This similar finding was true in the 1989 survey.

Table 1-10

Percentage of Those on Mailing List Who Gave at Least One Gift Per Year

Percent of Mailing List	Percent Who Gave a Gift	
	1994	1989
0-10	22.6	13.7
11-20	22.6	39.7
21-35	33.3	24.7
36-50	6.7	8.2
51-75	2.6	6.9
more than 75	0.0	0.0
not sure	12.0	6.9

In his study of 70 different Christian organizations, researcher James Engel (1983, pages 6, 7) states that the donor to nondonor ratio of a mailing list should not be less than 80/20. If it is, he would encourage substantial list cleaning to purge the list of the unproductive segment. It costs resource development budget dollars to continue to mail to nondonors who, for the most part, ignore the communications and would prefer their names be removed. If Engel's conclusions are applied to the Coalition for Christian Colleges & Universities institutions, remedial action should be taken by the majority of colleges who report a 50/50 ratio of donors to nondonors. The dilemma comes in desiring to maintain all alumni on the list even if they are unproductive, and one solution is greater segmentation and varying frequencies according to productivity.

Another consideration is what type of overall communication program has been implemented to cultivate that mailing list. The next chart, Table 1-11, gives a breakdown on the types of mailings sent and the frequency of those mailings during fiscal year 1993-94. College newsletters and magazines were sent the most frequently (some even monthly). There is little variation in the frequencies of communications during the five-year period.

Table 1-11
Number of Mailings

Type of Mailing	1994 High	1989 High	1994 Low	1989 Low	1994 Mean	1989 Mean
Newsletters/magazines	14	20	2	2	4.6	4.8
General appeals for funds	10	12	1	1	3.3	3.5
Segmented appeals:						
-major donors	12	12	1	1	2.5	2.8
-regular donors	12	16	1	1	2.7	2.9
-lapsed donors	6	5	1	1	2.1	1.8
-nondonors	4	4	1	1	1.9	1.7
-1st-time donor follow-up	12	12	1	1	2.6	2.2
-other	6	4	1	1	2.5	1.8

Knowledge of Constituency
Those concerned with developing the resources of an institution need to know its constituents—who they are and why they give. Knowing the audience is invaluable in order to communicate effectively, to market the college, and to educate the public. In addition, this step is necessary to gain a long-term view of the development process.

Constituent research and evaluation are the best means of accomplishing this. William Cumerford (1978, page 3) recommends a detailed and analytical survey to determine the basic facts as the first step in a development program. Of the responding colleges, however, only 45 percent conducted a market analysis of their donor constituencies in the last five years, but this was up from 38 percent in 1989. This means that just over half (55 percent) did not.

In the 1994 study, 35 percent of the colleges indicated that a survey was taken of their mailing list, up from 28 percent in 1989. The question asking why students attend their school was asked in 1985 and 1989 but not in 1994.

Funding the Budget—Who Pays?

Tuition funds approximately three-quarters (72 percent) of the Coalition for Christian Colleges & Universities' educational budgets—up from 66 percent five years earlier. Table 1-12 illustrates the percentage of each enrollment category's budget that comes from tuition: the smallest schools reported a mean of approximately 63 percent—up from 50 percent, and the largest at 78 percent—up from 74 percent.

The smallest schools, on the other hand, listed the highest mean percentage (21 percent) for gift income, while the larger schools posted the smallest mean percentage (6 percent). Overall mean for gift income is 12 percent—down from 17.1 percent five years ago. Clearly, institutions are becoming more tuition driven.

Endowments provide 3 percent of budget funding, and little divergency is reflected among the means reported in size categories (high of 4.4 percent to low of 2.2 percent). This is identical to five years ago. Individual schools attributed endowments with funding anywhere from 13 to 0 percent of their budgets.

"Other" sources of funding, such as auxiliary sales and services (bookstore, food, housing), church support, and government grants and aid, accounted for an overall mean of 13 percent, basically unchanged from five years ago. Means reported by size category range from 10 to 17 percent. Funding the Budget Figure 1-2 (1989) illustrates by graph the material displayed in Table 1-12.

Table 1-12

Funding the Budget: Percent of Education Budget Met by Size

Enrollment	Tuition		Gift Income		Endowment		Other	
	1994 Mean	1989 Mean	1994 Mean	1989 Mean	1994 Mean	1989 Mean	1994 Mean	1989 Mean
Up to 500	63	50	21	28	2	2	13	20
501-750	69	69	14	19	3	3	13	9
751-1000	74	64	12	17	4	4	10	15
1001-1250	71	70	12	15	4	2	15	11
1251-1500	72	73	10	12	2	3	15	13
1501-2000	76	69	6	10	3	1	17	18
2001+	78	74	8	9	4	3	11	13
Survey Mean	72	66	12	17	3	3	13	14

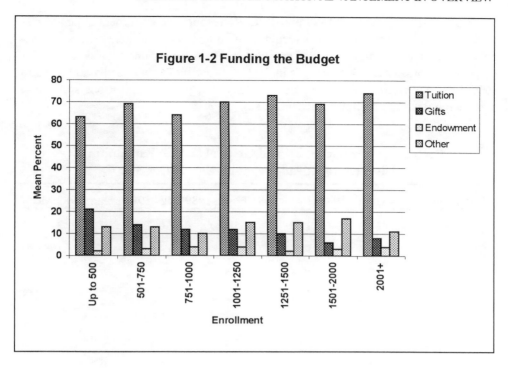

Figure 1-2 Funding the Budget

The Cost of Advancement

Table 1-13 exhibits the comparison of 1989 and 1994 survey respondents' total institutional expenditures (including salaries and benefits, travel, media/promotion, etc.) to perform admissions/recruitment, alumni affairs, fundraising, and public relations functions. Individual responses ranged from a low of $278,000 (in the up to 500 enrollment category) to a high of $3,135,647 (in the 2001+ enrollment category). Mean for the total survey population was $956,118.

Table 1-13
Advancement Expenditures by Enrollment Size

Enrollment	1994 High	1989 High	1994 Low	1989 Low	1994 Mean	1989 Mean
Up to 500	$702,500	$898,624	$278,000	$177,600	$481,307	$447,771
501-750	1,275,654	1,028,733	383,626	348,473	744,351	562,567
751-1000	1,736,436	1,203,473	510,629	369,766	815,661	628,640
1001-1250	1,428,814	1,119,542	491,160	547,000	987,306	853,797
1251-1500	1,583,952	1,347,541	561,096	514,270	962,046	845,614
1501-2000	2,103,954	2,381,560	747,000	490,787	1,194,587	1,360,417
2001+	3,135,647	2,324,100	739,277	490,000	1,921,578	1,323,451
Survey Mean of All Groups					$956,118	$772,028

Table 1-14 presents 1988-89 and 1993-94 resource development expenditures at the responding schools as a percentage of educational and general (E&G) expenditures. The overall average of population means for the entire sample was 9.3 percent in 1988-89 and 8.5 percent in 1993-94, and individual highs and lows in 1993-94 range from 16.8 to 4.3 percent. As you will note, institutions spend less percentage-wise as enrollment size increases.

Table 1-14
Percentage of Educational and General (E&G) Expenditures
Allocated to Advancement by Enrollment Size

Enrollment	1994 High	1989 High	1994 Low	1989 Low	1994 Mean	1989 Mean
Up to 500	15.4	31.0	5.9	7.0	10.6	13.2
501-750	16.8	14.3	7.5	6.4	11.3	10.0
751-1000	12.4	12.1	5.4	5.0	8.2	8.2
1001-1250	9.6	20.2	5.6	7.4	7.6	9.8
1251-1500	8.6	10.6	4.6	4.2	6.6	7.1
1501-2000	11.2	13.4	4.3	5.0	7.0	7.6
2001+	8.2	7.6	5.1	3.6	6.5	5.6
Survey Mean of All Groups					8.5	9.3

Breakdowns by the functions of admissions/recruitment, alumni development and public relations are provided in subsequent chapters. Figure 1-3 below, labeled 1994 Resource Development Expenditures by Enrollment Size, offers a quick overview of expenditures in each area. The proportionate change since 1989 is minimal and does not warrant notation.

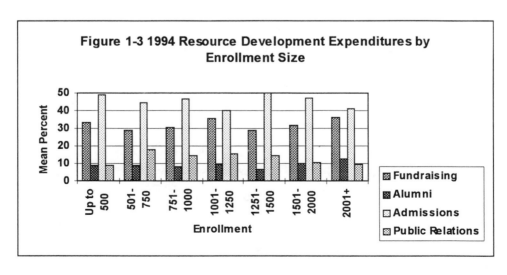

12

Personnel in Resource Development

Tables 1-15 and 1-16 reflect survey participants' responses to questions concerning total paid staff (FTE), professional and clerical/secretarial in their advancement offices. This overview of personnel data is further broken down into admissions/recruitment, alumni, development, and public relations categories in subsequent chapters.

Professional Staffing

Predictably, the number of advancement professionals generally tended to increase with enrollment size. Table 1-15 displays a range of individual highs and lows between 3 and 37 FTE, enrollment category means are between 7.8 and 18.7 FTE, and the overall survey mean, 12.0 FTE, is up slightly from 11.2 five years earlier.

Table 1-15
Number of Advancement Professionals (FTE) by Institutional Enrollment Size

Enrollment	1994 High	1989 High	1994 Low	1989 Low	1994 Mean	1989 Mean
Up to 500	12.0	16.5	4.25	5.0	7.8	8.0
501-750	13.1	12.0	7.0	4.0	9.9	9.0
751-1000	20.5	14.8	7.0	4.0	12.1	9.0
1001-1250	15.8	18.5	5.0	9.0	12.3	12.5
1251-1500	13.3	14.5	6.0	7.8	10.2	10.8
1501-2000	24.0	26.0	3.0	7.0	12.3	16.9
2001+	37.0	32.0	5.0	8.0	18.7	17.2
Survey Mean of All Groups					12.0	11.2

Clerical/Secretarial

The number of clerical/secretarial staff persons also tended to increase with enrollment in the 1994 survey. Table 1-16 shows individual highs and lows scattered between 2 and 20 FTE, enrollment category means between 3.6 and 10.6 FTE, and the overall survey mean at 6.2 FTE is comparable to the previous five years.

Table 1-16
Number of Clerical/Secretarial Personnel in Advancement (FTE)
by Institutional Enrollment Size

Enrollment	1994 High	1989 High	1994 Low	1989 Low	1994 Mean	1989 Mean
Up to 500	5.0	7.5	2.0	1.5	3.6	3.6
501-750	7.0	8.6	2.7	2.0	4.6	4.2
751-1000	10.0	8.5	2.0	2.5	5.4	5.4
1001-1250	11.0	11.0	2.0	4.0	6.3	7.3
1251-1500	11.0	9.0	2.0	4.0	6.6	7.1
1501-2000	12.0	16.0	4.0	5.0	7.6	8.6
2001+	20.0	23.0	4.0	3.0	10.6	10.1
Survey Mean of All Groups					6.2	6.0

Staff Increases

Thirty-nine (53 percent) of the 74 institutions who answered the question regarding staff growth said they planned to increase their resource development staff in the next two years (approximately the same percentage in 1989—49 percent). Twenty-one institutions (28 percent) responded they had no plans for expansion (up quite a jump from the 17 percent in 1989), and 14 (19 percent) reported they do not know whether or not they will expand in the next two years (a decrease from the 34 percent in 1989).

Of the 53 percent who reported they expect to increase their resource development staff, all but one said they will add professional staff. They projected their professional increases at a mean of 1.32 FTE, with the range between 1 and 3 FTE. Fifty-eight percent of those who plan to increase their professional staff (or 30 percent of total survey respondents) also will add clerical/secretarial staff. Their projected additions range between .5 and 2 FTE, with 1.1 FTE as the mean.

Sixty-two percent of the survey's respondents said they have increased their resource development staff in the last four years, with the average increase at 1.8 FTE and highs and lows between 8.5 and .5 FTE.

Use of Consultants

As observed in the earlier surveys, Christian colleges continued to use professional consultants for fundraising. Fewer have ventured into hiring consultants for admissions/recruitment, alumni affairs or public relations, respectively. Figure 1-4 indicates consultant use has fallen since 1984-85 in all areas.

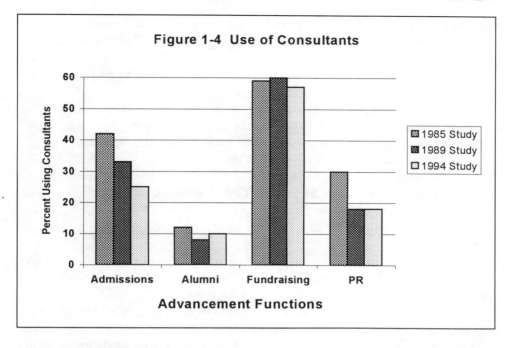

Figure 1-4 Use of Consultants

Professional Memberships

While they may not be increasing their use of consultants, many Coalition for Christian Colleges & Universities schools hold membership in a variety of professional organizations which offer opportunities for education, as well as networking and peer consulting. In the 1994 survey 75 percent of the institutions surveyed belonged to the Council for Advancement and Support of Education (CASE), 49 percent to the Christian Stewardship Association (CSA), 43 percent to the Association of Governing Board of Universities and Colleges (AGB), 43 percent to the National Society of Fund Raising Executives (NSFRE), 31 percent to the Evangelical Council for Financial Accountability (ECFA), and 9 percent to the Christian Management Association (CMA).

Tying It Together

Throughout this and the following chapters many facts, figures, and suggestions are displayed. Persons who try to follow the "rule of the book" will become frustrated and disillusioned unless they have developed a personal philosophy of resource development that guides the choices and priorities of their life and work.

Resource development is hard work, and it takes a toll on personnel and budgets. It often requires many long meetings, irregular hours, travel, and unrelenting correspondence. In the press of these activities, I try to keep before me the fact that the motivation for these activities is embodied in three concepts: faith, relationships, and service.

One of the uniquenesses of Christian college resource development professionals is the faith factor. Two major assumptions behind resource development for a Christian are divine ownership and human stewardship. We are never owners, but always stewards. We are only guardians of relations, strewards of time and talent, and trustees of possessions. God is the source of all the world's resources, and, as Psalms 24 tell us, he owns "everything in it." We do not own any assets because they are His, not ours, and our responsibility is to distribute God's assets.

At Christian institutions, the emphasis should be on opportunities, not just need. We must be careful not to get caught in a "their-money-for-our-ministry" mentality. Our responsibility is to provide opportunities for people to give as stewards of that which God has entrusted to them.

A balance between prayer and work, *or et labora*, then becomes pivotal to our efforts. Since our desire is to be used by God to accomplish His objectives, our planning and implementation is preceded and accompanied by prayer. Faith is a central concern to recognize that it is God who works in people's hearts, motivating them to give.

Our purpose is to promote understanding of the aims and objectives of our institutions among all our constituents that will encourage their prayer and financial support. Our plans should acknowledge our dependence on our Lord.

Accompanying our reliance on the Lord is our desire to develop and maintain long-term relationships with our constituents. Using the example of ministry mentioned in Philippians, fundraising most often occurs through existing relationships (1:1-8) and should seek involvement, not just token giving (4:14-16).

Within this context, all our communication (including letters, publications, phone calls, visits) is an effort to establish lifelong relationships built on honesty and integrity. Despite pressures to reach a particular goal, we are therefore committed to avoid manipulative techniques, to make full disclosure of our activities and receipts, and to be true to the values of our Christian faith.

Our concern is not only for a current need or this year's bottom line, but for developing long-term relationships with faithful supporters over a lifetime or until the Lord returns. This endeavor is a sacred trust that we should take most seriously.

A further look at the example in Philippians reveals that fundraising for the Christian is motivated by the spiritual benefit it provides the donor (4:17) and is an activity pleasing to God. Our objective should be to serve the needs of prospective donors in their stewardship: to provide giving opportunities through which they can distribute God's funds, to assist them in wise estate planning, to encourage Christian wills, and to provide counsel for current gifts consistent with their personal interests. Through these services, God's people are enabled to accomplish His work in their lives as they support our institutions. Hopefully, each of our efforts is but one more activity demonstrating our ministry partnership with loyal friends (Willmer, 1989, page 21).

Following these principles, I find a satisfaction in knowing that my efforts are part of a bigger plan that transcends my tenure in any particular position because it gives a framework to make decisions with confidence.

RESOURCES

Cumerford, William. **Fund Raising: a Professional Guide**. Ft. Lauderdale, FL: Ferguson E. Peters, 1978.

Hobbs, Walter C. and Francis, T. B. "On the Scholarly Activity of Higher Educationists," **Journal of Higher Education**, January 1973.

Engel, James. **Averting the Financial Crisis in Christian Organizations: Insights from a Decade of Donor Research**. Wheaton, IL: Management Development Associates, 1983.

Willmer, Wesley K. "Beyond Knee-jerk Thinking," **Case Currents**, January 1984.

Willmer, Wesley K., Ed. **Money for Ministries**, Wheaton, IL: Victor Books, 1989.

About the Author-Editor

WESLEY K. WILLMER is vice president of university advancement at Biola University in La Mirada, California, where he is responsible for enrollment management, alumni, university relations, marketing, development, and intercollegiate athletics. For additional information, please see "About the Author-Editor" following appendices.

Chapter 2

Presidents: Effective Fundraising Leadership

G. BLAIR DOWDEN

> "A distinguished faculty, fine students and good management are essential ingredients of a good college or university, but they depend on the availability of adequate resources" (Mullet, 1977, page 8).

Higher education is in the midst of the most difficult decade in 50 years. Slow economic growth, greater public outcry for accountability, rising vocationalism, emerging technologies, and changes in family finances have impacted colleges' and universities' fiscal health. Add to this "excess reliance on tuition income,...insufficient endowment relative to expenses, and a declining enrollment," (Hamlin and Hungerford, 1989, page 18) and one paints a fairly bleak picture.

Many commentators and researchers have documented the financial challenges faced by colleges and universities today. Dr. David Breneman, visiting professor of Harvard Graduate School of Education, commented: "After decades of remarkable expansion in size, scope, and resources, the outlook now is for much smaller growth" (1993, page 24).

Dr. Myron Augsburger, past president of the Coalition for Christian Colleges & Universities, observed that various external forces have brought the Christian college "into its most challenging time" (1994, page 1). Most commentators agree that the next decade will be one of tight budgets, lower enrollment, and substantial turmoil as colleges and universities seek to accomplish their missions within a rapidly changing environment.

What then should be higher education's response to these financial challenges? As every undergraduate business administration student will tell you, there are two ways to improve an organization's fiscal well-being: cut costs or enhance revenues. Many colleges have effectively reduced costs by reengineering processes and consolidating programs. Breneman states that the "focus in the foreseeable future must be on cost reduction" (1993, pages 24-25).

While cost reduction is often necessary, it is only effective to a point. Institutions must also work to enhance their revenues in order to maintain fiscal health and effectively accomplish their missions. Hamlin and Hungerford, in a study of

51 private colleges and universities experiencing severe financial crisis, found that those that successfully overcame their difficulties did so by enhancing revenue rather than decreasing expenditures (Hamlin and Hungerford, 1989, page 21).

Rodriguez agrees that enhancing revenue, and especially fundraising, is an important strategy for coping with the financial difficulties faced by many colleges and universities. He comments that this fact has changed the nature of the college presidency. "The role of the president is being redefined to an unfortunate degree by the financial difficulties many colleges face today—the financial cost of running private liberal arts colleges will increasingly oblige the president to spend more and more time and effort on securing non-tuition revenue" (1991, page 57).

Christian college presidents know this instinctively: programs cannot be developed, students graduated, equipment purchased, buildings constructed, or faculty hired without adequate resources. The dilemma comes with balancing competing priorities against the need to spend time, money, and attention on fundraising. Student problems, academic matters, enrollment concerns, and financial issues all clamor for consideration. And yet, experience shows that successful presidents are successful fund raisers.

Fundraising issues, problems, and pressures occupy a significant part of the schedules, thoughts, and energies of many college presidents. Consider the following typical scenarios:

- The senior development officer informs the president that he or she will need an additional $100,000 in his budget in order to meet fundraising goals. The development officer argues that an investment of $100,000 could yield additional giving of $500,000. The day previous to this request, the president had met with the academic dean to discuss eliminating several faculty positions in order to balance the budget.

- A new trustee, elected by the sponsoring denomination, calls the president aside following the completion of the new-trustee orientation session. During the orientation, the board chair emphasized the need for trustees to be actively involved in the fundraising process. This denominational trustee informs the president that he will not participate in the fundraising process. Further, he states that his only role on the board is to protect and preserve the denominational purity of the institution.

- A major donor calls the president early Monday morning. The donor just has been informed of the trustees' decision Saturday to change a traditional rule that has been in place since the college's founding. The week before, the president had spoken with him about a major gift of $3 million for the new physical education center. The major donor states that unless the trustee decision is reversed, he will withdraw his support.

- The senior development officer has scheduled an appointment for the president with a major New York City business executive and philanthropist. This busy executive already has cancelled two previous appointments. The president looks at his schedule to find this appointment conflicts with an important faculty meeting during which a critical vote on curricular changes will be taken. He feels a strong need to provide leadership in this important academic decision. However, if he cancels the donor meeting, he risks offending this individual and losing a potential major gift.

- A fundraising consultant informs the president that to be effective the institution should publish names of donors by gift levels. The consultant is a Christian and understands the evangelical nature of the institution. He feels that publishing donor lists is very appropriate and a necessary fundraising technique. The president has strong reservations about the appropriateness of the technique for a Christian institution.

These situations, though cast as fictional, are likely to be real in the life of a college president, given today's financial realities. They are typical of the decisions that a Christian college president faces as he or she seeks to raise funds. These dilemmas are difficult at best; they are no-win situations at worst. Yet, solutions can be found. Through effective leadership, a president can guide an institution past a quagmire of fundraising dilemmas and ultimately help it grow through increased financial support.

The importance of presidential leadership in fundraising has been well documented in the anecdotal and scholarly literature (Sammartino, 1982; West, 1983; Slinker, 1988; Dyson and Kirkman, 1989; Fisher and Quehl, 1989; Rodriguez, 1991; Felicetti, 1993; Cook, 1994; Janney, 1994). A 1989 Lilly Endowment-sponsored study reconfirmed and highlighted its importance. In a study of 10 public and private institutions that were highly effective in fundraising, Loessin and Duronio found that presidential leadership and participation in the fundraising process were the most important elements in determining fundraising effectiveness (1989). Commenting in the **Chronicle of Philanthropy,** Loessin stated: "Many people assumed that presidential leadership was important to development programs. What is entirely new here is how important it is. It turns out to be not [just] one of the factors, but by far the most important factor stimulating institutional advancement" (July 25, 1989, page 4).

Other commentators confirm the vital role that the president plays in fundraising. Slinker, in a study of 46 broadly representative public and private colleges found that "success in institutional advancement is the ultimate responsibility of the president" (1988, page 4). Some would say that fundraising is *the* most important presidential role. "People may judge your success as CEO more on your skill in attracting private support than any other aspect of leadership" (Costello, 1993, page 25).

Whether the most important role or just an important role, all commentators agree that successful fundraising does not occur unless the president is actively involved. Cook, in a national study of 50 university presidents, stated that "presidents no longer have a choice in whether or not to engage in fund raising" (1994, page 2). Ness notes that the presidential role in fundraising cannot be delegated to others.

> "It is the function of development...which seems most inescapably to fall to the responsibility of the president. He or she can—and usually does—engage a chief development officer who, with any luck, is experienced, compatible, and possessed of a Midas touch. Yet in no sense does this acquisition relieve the president of primary and comprehensive responsibility for the development needs of the institution. Presidential leadership is a sine qua non" (1975, page V).

Presidents come in all shapes and sizes and with a variety of backgrounds, experiences, and interests. They are female and male, young and old, ordained ministers or lay people, business persons or educators. Their institutions are small or large, have significant or small endowments, have graduate programs or are baccalaureate only, are denominationally affiliated or independent. While these factors vary, the ways in which a president exerts fundraising leadership does not change from president to president or institution to institution. Consider the following tasks, in all of which a president's leading can be critical. These tasks will serve as a framework for this discussion on presidential leadership in fundraising:

1. Articulate clear vision, mission, and goals.
2. Serve as chief development officer.
3. Focus on highest potential prospects.
4. Develop, train, and motivate trustees as fundraisers and as institutional spokespersons.
5. Select a high-quality senior development officer.
6. Develop an effective working relationship with the senior development officer.
7. Allocate sufficient resources for the development function.
8. Seek out educational opportunities in fundraising.
9. Consider, discuss, and encourage integration of Christian faith and fundraising practices.
10. Demonstrate integrity in fundraising tasks.

Research in higher education confirms the importance of presidential leadership in fundraising. What follows is a list of practical guidelines for developing and maintaining effective presidential fundraising leadership. While application of the guidelines will differ among institutions due to campus climate and presidential personality, the principles remain the same and are fundamental to fundraising effectiveness and ultimately to institutional success.

1. Articulate clear vision, mission, and goals.
Presidents have multiple roles to perform on the higher education stage: visionary, financier, encourager, leader, and servant. Among these, perhaps the most important role is that of setting and articulating the institutional vision. Theodore Hes-

burgh, former president of Notre Dame, comments: "The most important contribution a president can make to institutional advancement is to articulate his vision of the institution so persistently and persuasively that it becomes shared by all constituents... who adopt it as their own" (Rodriguez, 1991, page 67).

Nanus, in his significant book, **Visionary Leadership**, defines vision as "a realistic, credible, attractive future for your organization" (1992, page 8). He states that vision accomplishes several things in an organization:

- the right vision attracts commitment and energizes people
- the right vision creates meaning in workers' lives
- the right vision establishes a standard of excellence
- the right vision bridges the present and the future (1992, pages 16-17).

Vision is essential to effective fundraising leadership. Without it an advancement program cannot be successful. Costello comments: "Vision and leadership—these are the most essential elements in a successful advancement program. It is the president's well-articulated vision of where the institution can go that excites faculty, students, staff, alumni, donors, and friends" (1993, page 25).

For Christian college presidents, vision building must begin with significant meditation and prayer in order to discover God's plans for the college or university, for, if God is not in the vision, it is doomed to fail. David C. LeShana, president of Western Evangelical Seminary notes, "An institution without a dream or vision...is characterized by a sense of drifting and a lack of expectation. But if we are to move beyond mediocrity and aimlessness, we need to capture God's dream of what He wants to do in and through our corporate lives" (1988, page 118).

Like clear vision, a clear mission is also essential for presidential effectiveness in fundraising. Vision expresses where an institution is going. A mission statement explains why it makes the journey. The mission statement should clearly and concisely describe the *raison d'etre* of the institution. A person unfamiliar with the institution, by reading this statement, should be able to determine the institution's historical roots, purposes, publics served, and programs. The development of such a statement is the responsibility of the president.

In creating a mission statement, the president should ensure that a variety of internal and external constituencies, including faculty, staff, administration, students, alumni, trustees, major donors, and others, have an opportunity to review and revise the document. To be effective, the mission statement must be owned by the constituencies. Once adopted, the mission statement should be widely circulated by means of institutional publications.

Successful fundraising does not occur without a clearly developed mission statement. Neff comments: "More fund raising prospects falter because of the institution's failure to present a clear mission than for any other factor" (1993, page 92).

A president must be able to clearly articulate the institutional mission in order to cultivate financial support. A carefully developed mission statement sets an institution apart from its competitors. A clearly communicated mission makes a school unique in the mind of the donor. Hurtubise, in a study of eight select small independent liberal arts colleges and universities in the San Francisco Bay area, found that "to cultivate financial support, a president must be able to articulate the institution's mission and goals" (1988, page 2).

A clear vision and a clear mission lead to clear goals for the institution and for fundraising endeavors. Development of clear goals requires a systematic strategic planning process. Vaccaro argues: "The need for strategic planning has never been greater, especially for the church-related institution, which must labor under difficult conditions of diminishing enrollments, intensive competition from larger state colleges and universities, and a lack of endowment sufficient to produce a 'safety net' during times of contraction and retrenchment " (1988, page 75). He suggests a seven-step strategic planning process.

1. Identifiy, clarifiy, and articulate the college's mission and purpose.

2. Identify specific goals and objectives to fulfill the mission and purpose.

3. Identify programs and courses necessary to meet the goals and objectives.

4. Identify the resources necessary for implementing courses and programs.

5. Analyze and compare resources needed to resources available.

6. Develop a series of one-year budgets to identify the allocation of available resources to the agreed-upon programs.

7. Plan and develop a system for periodic evaluation of the plan (Vacarro, 1988, page 78).

Once an institutional strategic plan has been developed, fundraising plans can be developed to fulfill the institutional plan. Fundraising is not a function in itself, but a method of helping the institution achieve its plans and objectives. As Manning notes, an institutional plan is "an aid to fund raising, it provides a guide to the kinds of gifts needed and the ways they will be used to further the work of the institution" (Nelson, 1986, page 46).

The president needs to take leadership in developing fundraising strategic plans. Slinker argues: "Proper advancement strategy can be decisive for a president and institution in realizing the college or university mission" (1988, page *iii*).

In his study of 46 colleges and universities, Slinker found that presidents are actively involved in setting long range fundraising plans. Fifty-six percent establish such plans annually with 37 percent establishing them at least twice a year (1988, page 101). In addition, 63 percent of the presidents work monthly with the advancement staff in establishing short-range goals and objectives, with 19 percent establishing such goals on a weekly basis (1988, page 104).

Slinker concludes that effective presidents "formulate an advancement strategy that reflects where the institution has been and where it is now and where it wants to go" (1988, page 178).

Clear vision, mission, and goals precede successful fundraising endeavors. A strategic long-range plan derives from the mission and vision; fundraising plans will be based on the strategic long-range plan. Experience shows that, without a clear sense of vision, mission, and goals, the institution's fundraising will suffer. The effective president champions the vision and mission and, through fundraising, turns visions and plans into reality.

2. Serve as chief development officer.

> "To be successful in fund raising, a president must learn to ask for money and not leave the task entirely to trustees, volunteers, or staff. Few development programs are effective without the commitment, leadership, and participation of a strong president" (Fisher, 1984, page 164).

The president should have active and primary involvement in fundraising to ensure institutional success. Indeed, experience shows that he or she should be the chief fund raiser for the institution. One commentator ranked fundraising as the number one responsibility of a college president (West, 1983, page 13). Another described it as the "grandest of presidential responsibilities" (Fisher, 1989, page 31). And another stated that "college presidents are the central decision makers and strategists in fund raising" (Anderson, 1984, page 17). In spite of this, many presidents feel ambivalent about their fundraising role. West reflects these feelings: "I would prefer to put educational leadership or spending time with students or long-range planning ahead of fund raising, but the truth of the matter is that, however well a small-college president does all those things, his tenure probably will be short if he cannot raise money" (1983, page 13).

Priority given to a task may be judged by hours spent on the task. By this measure, a 1989 study of 77 Coalition for Christian Colleges & Universities presidents revealed that they considered fundraising and related advancement activities as one of their most important responsibilities (Dowden, 1990, page 25). The presidents indicated that they spent an average of 44 percent of their time in fundraising, advancement, and public relations functions, in contrast to 21 percent on academic affairs, 21 percent on financial affairs, and 14 percent on student development. (See Figure 2-1.)

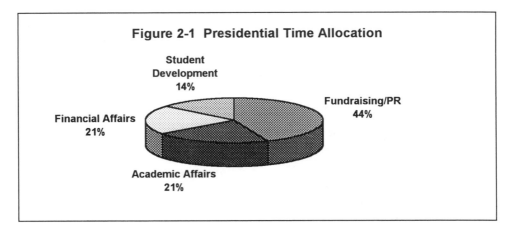

Figure 2-1 Presidential Time Allocation

Student Development 14%

Fundraising/PR 44%

Financial Affairs 21%

Academic Affairs 21%

Coalition presidents were also asked to specify how they spent that portion of their time devoted to development/advancement/public relations activities. (See Figure 2-2.) Presidents indicated that 40 percent of that time was spent in fundraising, with the remainder allocated to public relations (24 percent), admissions (13 percent), alumni affairs (12 percent), and other advancement activities (11 percent).

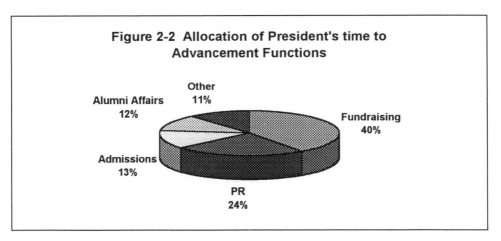

Figure 2-2 Allocation of President's time to Advancement Functions

Other 11%

Alumni Affairs 12%

Fundraising 40%

Admissions 13%

PR 24%

Other studies support the 1989 Coalition findings that presidents spend a significant amount of time on fundraising activities. Slinker concludes: "Fund raising is one of the top priorities for the college and university presidents—and will receive greater attention in future years" (1988, page 129). His study found that among respondents, 63 percent of the presidents rate their involvement in fundraising as high, with 33 percent rating it as moderate. When asked how much involvement they desired in the future, 73 percent of the presidents wanted high involvement and 27 percent desired moderate involvement (1988, pages 88, 89).

Given the amount of time that presidents, and specifically Christian college presidents, spend on fundraising, it is surprising to discover the amount of ambivalence and, in some cases, outright hostility, exhibited toward this task. In the 1989 study, several Coalition presidents rejected their role as chief fundraising officer and indicated they delegated that task to the senior development officer. One commented: "I am deeply troubled about my role as a fund raiser, troubled that the outside world sees me as a fund raiser rather than as a totality of my responsibilities as a Christian educator." Another commented: "Fund raising used to be the seventh or eighth priority on the list of qualifications for president. Now, at a Christian college, it is number two, right after being a Christian." Another noted: "I view myself as the chief fund raiser for my institution, but I wish I did not have to. I look forward to the day when this is not true."

Several Coalition presidents felt that fundraising kept them from exerting institutional leadership. These presidents wanted to be able to spend more time in shaping academic programs. One stated: "I feel the academic side demands much more attention than it is getting. The key to good fund raising is a good academic program."

In contrast, several Coalition presidents felt that their role in fundraising helped rather than hindered their ability to shape an institution and enhance their leadership. One noted: "Presidents must bring in the large institution-changing gifts. These gifts do shape the values of the institution and provide a vehicle for leadership." Fisher, Tack, and Wheeler concur in their book, **The Effective College President**. They note that a lack of resources can hinder a president's effectiveness and exercising of leadership (1988, pages 91, 92).

Conversations with several presidents during the 1989 study indicated that those who had been in their positions for a longer period of time had a more positive view of the importance of presidential leadership in fundraising. In contrast, those who had been in the presidency for a brief period of time and came from a non-development background tended to resent the fundraising role and have a negative opinion of it. They felt that fundraising prevents them from exercising leadership rather than helps them in their institutional leadership role.

One of the constraints preventing presidents from fulfilling their chief fundraiser role is the tension felt between fundraising needs and other institutional priorities. Indeed, an increased role in fundraising often necessitates a reduced role in other leadership areas at the college. Rodriguez notes: "As the president's role in fund raising increases, other roles tend to receive less attention. Specifically, there is noticeably less president involvement in student and faculty affairs today compared with prior eras" (1991, page 2).

Many Coalition presidents in 1989 reported great pressure from time constraints. These constraints have not ameliorated since 1989 and, if anything, have been heightened due to increased financial pressures. Coalition presidents indicated that, while they wanted to be more involved in the fundraising process, they felt that the time they spent on other institutional priorities prevented them from doing this. Fisher noted and sympathized with this dilemma, yet emphatically dismissed this excuse. "No responsibility is more important to presidential success [than fundraising]. Yet many presidents rationalize by saying that they are bogged down with more important matters on campus or that they are just plain uncomfortable dealing with off-campus people and conditions..." (1984, pages 121,122).

Research has demonstrated that presidential involvement in fundraising does lead to greater success. Rodriguez, in his study of 217 chief development and advancement officers, found that there is "a statistically significant relationship between success in alumni donor participation rates and college presidents who frequently open their house to alumni couples, speak to alumni on the theme of fortifying the historical values of the college, and include on their top donor cultivation list seven or more alumni or alumni spouses" (1991, page *ii*).

Slinker, in his study on the role of the college president in institutional advancement, found that "presidential procrastination in institutional advancement victimizes the potential of the college or university, stranding the president or institution on a road to mediocrity or failure" (1988, page 155).

Slinker also found that "college and university presidents share a common belief that their role in institutional advancement has an impact on their presidency" (1988, page 85). Eighty-five percent of the presidents in the sample group indicated that it was highly important for the president to be involved in advancement programs in order for the institution to be successful with constituencies (1988, page 94).

Janney, in a 1994 study of Coalition for Christian Colleges & Universities presidents and their fundraising effectiveness, observed that "skillful and enthusiastic presidential involvement may be the key to a successful college fund raising program" (1994, page 8). His study concluded that fundraising effectiveness was related to a president's administrative style. Presidents with an open style, that is, those who "believe in the value of one on one meetings, work long hours, are warm and affable, care deeply about the welfare of the individual, and encourage creative types," are more effective in their fundraising than those with less open administrative styles (Janney, 1994, page 5).

If presidential involvement as chief development officer is critical to institutional fundraising success, what is the president's responsibility in raising dollars for a college or university? The presidential fundraising role includes the following:

- Approve, monitor, and evaluate all fundraising plans, objectives, and timetables. Even the best development office needs to be accountable for meeting objectives.

- Spend a significant amount of time with major donors and prospects. In typical fundraising efforts, 20 percent of the donors give 80 percent of the gifts. The 20 percent includes the individuals who the president must personally contact and solicit for gifts. The work of visiting, inspiring, and soliciting these major donors should not be delegated. The institution's success, the success of the fundraising effort, and the president's success depend on it.

- Work to ensure adequate internal support for the fundraising plan and development personnel. Often there is a natural, but unhealthy, suspicion of fundraising and development officers among faculty and staff. Frequently, development officers are seen as individuals who have expensive dinners, travel in luxury cars, glad-hand people, and manipulate for gifts to the institution. The president can, through word and deed, support the development staff and clearly articulate the method and manner of the fundraising process. A wide and regular dissemination of information regarding fundraising plans, programs, purposes, and results will help tear down the barriers of suspicion.

Slinker, based on his study of presidential fundraising effectiveness, lists several tasks that presidents should undertake to ensure sufficient funds for their institutions.

1. Establish robust and proactive leadership as a priority.

2. Lead with enthusiasm, strength, vitality, honest and ethical convictions, a vision to inspire others, and teamwork.

3. Formulate an advancement strategy that reflects where the institution has been, where it is now, and where it wants to go.

4. Chair the planning committee and involve advancement staff members.

5. Clearly define and base educational goals and objectives on the institutional mission.

6. Abstain from personal involvement in time intensive projects or activities.

7. Hire and retain the best professionals in the field.

8. Delegate the responsibility and coordination of advancement functions to an executive officer.

9. Provide advancement budgets to achieve goals, objectives, and the institutional mission.

10. Generate a feeling in donors that they have a special institutional ownership.

11. Be open to communicate change (1988, pages 177-183).

Presidential involvement in fundraising is critical. Bishop and Hurtubise advise presidents that, although they are "at the vertex of the institutional hierarchy, they must simultaneously be at the center of the institution's fundraising efforts—creating, motivating, evaluating, and soliciting" (1991, page 33).

3. Focus on highest potential prospects.

"The single most important component of any educational institution's development strategy is major gift fund raising" (Cosovich, 1993, page 1).

To be successful, presidents must focus their scarce time resources on the most important priorities. In fundraising, that means placing priority attention and time on the cultivation and solicitation of major gift prospects. Vilfredo Pareto, noted Italian mathematician, postulated that 80 percent of any result comes from 20 percent of the effort. Pareto's Law, as it has come to be known, helps to guide and prioritize our fundraising. Because we know that, routinely, 80 percent of the gifts come from 20 percent of the donors, it follows that 80 percent of the fund-raising efforts should be directed to this 20 percent of the donors. This is, perhaps, one of the more important guidelines for presidential fundraising success: focus energies and attention on the highest potential projects and prospects that will bring the most gifts to the institution. As Boardman notes: "If the president does not devote ample time to advancing the [major] gift process, then the program is destined to fail" (1993, page 80).

Successful fundraising presidents effectively cultivate and solicit major donor prospects. Cook, in his study of the role of university presidents and chancellors in fundraising, found that because "presidents are instrumental in raising a major part of the private support for the universities" (1994, page 2), they should "focus their effort and attention in fund raising on major gifts and administrative leadership" (1994, page 1).

Felicetti, in a 1991 study of Council of Independent Colleges member institutions, found that presidents spend "59 percent of their total fund-raising time on cultivating and soliciting major donors" (1993, page 77). Further, when they meet with their senior development officers, they discuss major donors more often than any other topic (1993, page 77).

Effective fundraising presidents spend priority time cultivating and soliciting high potential prospects, and, according to Brown, "actually enjoy donor prospect cultivation—the planning, the approach, and, yes, even the asking. They strongly believe in their vision and are confident that others will also" (1988, page 150).

While the process of obtaining a major gift through one-on-one cultivation and solicitation is fairly simple, implementation of the process is anything but simple. It requires persistence, hard work, time, and opportunity. It also demands presidential involvement and a strong working relationship with the senior development officer. Yet the joys are immeasurable. Dailey lists seven steps to a major gift:

1. Prospect identification.

2. Research and qualification.

3. Strategizing the approach.

4. Involving the prospect.

5. Making the ask.

6. Closing the solicitation.

7. After-solicitation follow-up (1986, page 82).

A useful concept for presidents to consider, in thinking about major gift solicitation, is Smith's "Five I's of Fundraising," commonly referred to as the cultivation cycle (Figure 2-3) (1986, page 325).

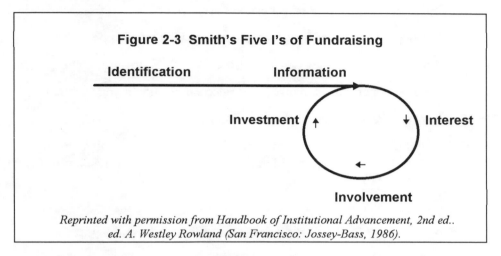

Figure 2-3 Smith's Five I's of Fundraising

Identification   **Information**

Investment   **Interest**

Involvement

Reprinted with permission from Handbook of Institutional Advancement, 2nd ed..
ed. A. Westley Rowland (San Francisco: Jossey-Bass, 1986).

Smith says that to cultivate and solicit a major donor properly, one needs to move from the identification of that donor to providing information about the institution, developing an interest and involving the prospect in institutional activities and governance, and, finally, asking for an investment in the institution. The time from identification to investment will vary for each prospect; it can be as short as a few months or as long as several years. However long it takes, each step in the cycle is important in encouraging major donor gifts (1986, page 305). Presidential involvement will sometimes come at the identification stage, but often comes at the involvement and investment stage.

Involvement is an important element in cultivating and soliciting major donors. Presidents can be key in providing this involvement by asking prospects to be involved in the institution through service on an advisory or governance board, through teaching or lecturing, through assistance in the fundraising process or in other ways. Cook found: "The primary forms of donor involvement used by presidents include invitation to campus activities and events, and membership on advisory councils and boards of trustees" (1994, page 2).

The place in the cultivation cycle that is often the most difficult—asking for the gift—is the most important. Usually people don't give if they haven't been asked. Presidents need to be actively involved in the solicitation process, especially with higher level prospects. A 1991 survey of the members of the Council of Independent Colleges (CIC) found that $1,000+ donors were most often solicited by staff (46.4 percent) and the president (32 percent) (Dowden, 1993, page 54).

The national consulting firm, Gonser Gerber Tinker and Stuhr, in their periodic bulletin, **Bulletin on Public Relations and Development**, lists 10 components which provide for success in obtaining major gifts:

1. Be sure that obtaining major gifts is a team effort.

2. Be sure that your case for support is dramatic and compelling.

3. Insist that senior development officers are involved in the effort.

4. Develop strategies for building relationships with major prospects.

5. Regularly review and update your list of major gift prospects.

6. Develop opportunities to involve prospects in the life of your institution.

7. Promote dreams, ideas, and plans—not needs.

8. Listen to your prospects—they have much to say about their interest in your institution, about their families, and about issues which are of great importance to them.

9. Provide attention, honor, gratitude, and recognition to major donors.

10. Publicize gifts of major dimension (September 1993, pages 2-4).

Major gifts are important and essential to the fiscal health of an institution. Experience and research shows that successful major gift efforts are led by presidents. Presidents must provide the time, energy, motivation, and vision to ensure that major gifts are secured, and they must focus priority time from their crowded schedules to the care and feeding of the highest potential prospects.

4. Develop, train, and motivate trustees as fundraisers and as institutional spokespersons.

> "Without substantial help from the governing board, institutions cannot be expected to reach the sizeable fund raising goals they set for themselves. The chief executives simply cannot do it alone" (Gale, 1989, page 102).

The trustee's role in the fundraising process is extremely important. This fact is documented in several other chapters in this book. Unless trustees play an active role in the fundraising process, institutions have difficulty raising a significant number of major gifts. To be effective in fundraising, trustees need to give of their own resources and inspire others to give. The effective president should recruit, develop, train, and motivate trustees who can take an active leadership role in fundraising.

Research confirms the importance of trustee participation in fundraising. Bishop and Hurtubise, in their 1988 study, found that "the successful fund raising president believes [that one of] the most important roles for the trustees is to contribute financially to the institution..." (1988, pages 33, 34). Davis found a link between institutional quality and board commitment to fundraising: "the 'common denominator' contributing to the institutional growth and quality was a strong board of trustees committed to quality advancement" (Brown, 1988, page 147).

Experienced presidents also know the importance of active board involvement in fundraising. Broce, former college president and foundation executive, believes that "a committed 'governing board' that accepts ownership of the fund raising program" is one of three basic criteria for successful fundraising along with having fundraising goals based on institutional needs and employing a quality development staff. He states: "Governing boards can make or break fund raising" (page 1). Dr. Norman A. Wiggins, president of Campbell University, puts it even more strongly. "If your trustees do not help you to secure funds, freshmen, and friends, yours is a crippled institution and often a lost cause" (1988, page 4). Robert W. Neff, president of Juniata College, in a 1991 survey of Council of Independent Colleges, concluded that trustee giving is essential. "The trustees' willingness to give sets the margin of difference for an institution" (1993, page 97). He states unequivocally: "The board's role in advancement is critical" (1993, page 91).

Presidents often express frustration with their trustees' role in the fundraising process as illustrated by the Coalition presidents who were surveyed in 1989. While most of these presidents felt that trustees should give to the institution and identify, cultivate, and solicit major donors, most also felt that this was not occurring. One stated: "Trustees should lead in giving and sharing with others regarding the institution; and in bringing in contacts; they should, but they don't." Another said: "I would love to have more fund raisers on my board, but don't have them." Most presidents felt that their boards were inadequately prepared for the fundraising role.

The 1991 survey of 247 Council of Independent Colleges institutions also found a degree of dissatisfaction with boards' training and involvement in fundraising. Eighty-five percent of the CIC colleges noted that "their trustees were not adequately trained in fund raising" (Neff, 1993, page 103). In addition, there was a high degree of dissatisfaction with trustees giving or getting financial resources. Only 30 percent of the responding institutions were very satisfied or satisfied with board giving, and only 15 percent were very satisfied or satisfied with the board member's role in soliciting new donors. In contrast, 34 percent expressed dissatisfaction in trustee giving and 44 percent expressed dissatisfaction in the trustee's role in soliciting new donors (Neff, 1993, page 103).

Good trusteeship begins with good recruiting. Many presidents are hampered in these efforts. In the 1989 study, Coalition presidents expressed significant frustration in recruiting trustees. Seventy-three percent indicated some difficulty in recruiting trustees, with 50 percent indicating moderate or extreme difficulty. Recruiting good fundraising trustees is particularly difficult in denominationally-affiliated schools where trustees are nominated and approved by external boards or regional church bodies, many times hindering the identification of individuals who can exert leadership in fundraising. Even in schools without denominational affiliation, it is difficult at best to recruit quality trustees.

In spite of these roadblocks to recruiting, a president must exert leadership in this area. Presidents of denominationally-affiliated institutions might consider encouraging external denominational boards to weigh the importance of fundraising expertise when selecting trustees and should attempt to gain a voice in the selection process. Presidents of colleges with self-perpetuating boards should work with board committees to identify and select those individuals who can have a strong and positive effect on fundraising and friend raising.

Obviously, board membership should not be exclusively reserved for the wealthy. Boards need to be diverse in nature and background. Individuals with expertise in academics, law, business, education, and ministry need to be selected. Further, boards should represent a geographical and ethnic mix and balance. A significant portion of the trustees should be able to contribute substantially to the institution and encourage others to do likewise. All should be encouraged to give as part of their responsibilities, no matter how small the gift may be.

The effective president not only identifies excellent trustees, but also develops, trains, and motivates these trustees. This means providing orientation programs for new trustees and periodic fundraising workshops for continuing trustees. Coalition presidents in 1989 suggested several methods of board fundraising training:

1. Outside "experts" to speak with the board in a retreat setting

2. Board seminars

3. Video presentations

4. Board seminars with president and development staff members

5. Weekend retreats

The trustee training method most frequently recommended by Coalition presidents was a retreat setting where a Christian speaker/facilitator works with the board on fundraising concerns. As one Coalition president stated: "Such retreats help to raise the consciousness level of trustees regarding their role."

The effective fundraising president encourages board participation in the fundraising process. To demand less from one's trustees could result in not reaching institutional potential.

5. Select a high-quality senior development officer.

> "After the appointment of the president, the appointment of the chief development officer is the single factor that most affects fund raising results" (MacMillan, 1990, page 65).

Effective college presidents select high-quality individuals to lead the development effort. This is often easier said than done. Presidents frequently find it difficult to recruit development officers who will fit within their institutions. Scarcity of quality, experienced personnel has heightened the competition for educational fund raisers. The unique nature of Christian institutions further narrows the field of available applicants.

Coalition presidents, in the 1989 study, identified several qualifications that are important in hiring a senior development officer. These qualifications, listed from most important to least important, are:

Table 2-1

Qualifications for Hiring a Chief Development Officer

Rank	Qualification
1	General leadership ability
2	Planning and management skills
3	Previous experience in development
4	Communication skills
5	Denominational/doctrinal qualifications
6	Philosophy of fundraising
7	Previous experience in Christian higher education
8	History with the institution
9	Advanced degree

Slinker identified a similar list of characteristics in his study of 46 institutions. Important characteristics valued by presidents in their development staff included (listed in descending order of importance) initiative, creativity, professional competence, interpersonal skills, cooperation, effectiveness in dealing with constituents, frankness in dealing with others, responsibility, and tact (1988, pages 111-113). MacMillan offers these words of advice, in hiring a senior development officer: "Think young, think 'family,' think direct experience—even if this experience has been limited" (1990, page 66).

The search for a senior development officer is, perhaps, the most difficult senior administrative search. Robert W. Dingman, in a survey of fundraising consultants, notes several reasons for this difficulty (1995):

1. Unreal expectations regarding the development officer's function

2. Lack of a balanced philosophy and theology of fundraising

3. Lack of commitment by the president and trustees to fundraising and development

4. Demand exceeds supply of qualified candidates.

In any search, preparation is the key. This becomes essential in searching for a position where so few qualified candidates exist. Martha Stachitas, senior vice president-executive search, at Barnes and Roche, Inc., suggests a three-stage process in a search for a senior development officer. First, the president should define the position. What is needed and wanted in a senior development officer, and what qualifications are necessary? Second, the president should identify appropriate candidates. It is important that there be a personality fit with the president as well as an institutional fit. Stachitas advises that presidents "do a chemistry test" with the candidate pool. Third, the president needs to be aggressive in recruiting the individual to the college (1995).

In searching for a senior development officer, Dingman recommends that presidents ask the following questions:

- Is this person proactive and not behind the desk most of the time?
- Has this candidate asked for and received major gifts?
- Is there ample evidence of excellent relationship-building skills?
- Does the candidate have strengths that will parallel my needs?
- Is this a person I could travel with?
- Can I trust this person and will he/she maintain a confidence?
- Does this person's theology of stewardship match mine?
- What are the minimal requirements that this candidate would make of me as president? (Dingman, 1995).

The search for an appropriate senior development officer is time consuming, but vitally important. It should be undertaken with much thought, prayer, and work. This is especially true, given the high rate of turnover of senior development officers. During the years 1984 through 1992, 22 percent of senior development officers left their jobs each year. This translates into an average tenure of 4.6 years (Mooney, 1993, page A16). MacMillen found, in a 1989 study, that the average tenure of senior development officers in Coalition institutions was 3.65 years (1990, page 65).

Effective presidents are careful, systematic, and prayerful in selecting senior development officers and choose individuals with whom they feel comfortable. Personality fit is as important in this selection process as is institutional fit. The rewards of a proper selection are great, and a well-chosen senior development officer can ease the fundraising burden. Without a proper selection, frustrations mount, hampering effective fundraising efforts. Effective presidential leadership in fundraising depends on the selection of a high-quality senior development officer.

6. Develop an effective working relationship with the senior development officer.

"A special functional relationship must exist between the president and the institutional advancement officers" (Rowland, 1977, page 529).

A close working relationship between the president and the senior development officer is essential. The relationship must be one built on integrity, mutual respect, trust, and a personal chemistry (Cook, 1994, page 4). In addition, the president and the senior development officer must have a similarity in their approach and attitudes toward fundraising. Moore, in a study of 200 four-year, independent, undergraduate colleges, found that presidents and senior development officers that demonstrate a high level of similarity in goals and approaches raise more money and enjoy it more (1987, pages 40-44).

An effective working relationship between the president and the senior development officer is particularly important due to the numerous hours spent together.

When Coalition presidents were asked, in the 1989 survey, how frequently they met with their senior development officers, 91 percent reported daily or weekly meetings. During those meetings, according to Coalition presidents, more than one third of the time was spent discussing major donor contacts with an additional one fourth of the time spent discussing general fundraising issues. The remainder was devoted to discussion of general administrative issues, public relations matters, and other items. Similar time allocations were indicated by respondents to the 1991 survey of CIC colleges (Felicetti, 1993, page 77).

Given the essential nature of the president-senior development officer relationship, what should a president expect of a senior development officer? Likewise, what should a senior development officer expect of a president? In a series of articles in **CASE Currents** (November-December 1993), Steven Trachtenberg, Kathryn Costello, and Mark Fisher comment on mutual expectations in the president-senior development officer relationship. Trachtenberg notes, based on his 18 years of experience as a college president, that senior development officers should have the following qualities: loyalty, honesty, shared enthusiasm, assertiveness, efficiency, ability to provide support, good program management, ability to work alone as well as with the president, good focus, and approachability (1993, pages 19-22). Fisher adds that the senior development officer must develop a mutually supportive relationship with the president, one that is characterized by "total candor" and open communication (Fisher, 1993, pages 36-42).

Likewise, senior development officers have the right to expect certain things from the other half of the fundraising team. Costello describes presidential qualities that contribute to a strong fundraising partnership between the president and senior development officer: vision and leadership, commitment to the campus, commitment to advancement, integrity, honesty, perseverance, patience, optimism, communication skills, energy, openness to advice, humor, creativity, willingness to ask for money, and managerial ability (1993, pages 25-28).

One of the most important, and perhaps one of the most difficult, aspects of the presidential-senior development officer relationship is the matter of time. Presidents must be willing to allocate sufficient time resources to effectively meet fundraising goals and objectives. Likewise, senior development officers need to manage carefully that portion of a president's time devoted to development. Fisher quotes Rita Bornstein, president of Rollins College, regarding how a senior development officer can most effectively schedule the president's time. "Work closely with his or her office staff to arrange meetings and events around trips already planned for other presidential business. Manage your CEO's time wisely on trips out of town, neither leaving too much space between visits nor overcrowding the schedule" (1993, page 40). Adams recommends that presidents "let their senior development officers program them somewhat" (1989, page 18).

A helpful way for the senior development officer to make the most of the president's time is by developing a priority contact chart, as illustrated in Figure 4. It is recommended that this chart be reviewed and updated in weekly meetings between the president and senior development officer. The chart serves as a scheduling guide for the president and his/her secretary. It also serves as a way for the senior development officer to hold the president accountable for important fundraising contacts.

Figure 2-4 Presidential Contacts—May

	Prospect Name	Strategy/Action Steps	Asking Amount
1.	May visits John Rees (Jane) 5 E. 79th St. New York, NY 10028 (212) 777-2356 (home) (212) 555-1212 (office)	—discuss potential dates for visit —present proposal for $300,000 —funding of academic chair	$300,000
	Jeff Toben (Betty) Hampton, NY 11927 (516) 324-1111 (home) (516) 324-3656 (office)	—visit in May —ask for $2.5 million gift ($1 million for academic chair and $1.5 million for fine arts center)	$2.5 million
2.	Important calls/letters to write Don Jones (Joan) 19 Aloe Court Sun City, AZ 85351 (602) 222-1111 (home)	—write to document solicitation for $10,000 toward fine arts project. This would be in addition to current pledge of $15,000.	$10,000
	Ken Bonner 365 Ocean Lockport, NY 14045 (716) 421-2345	—call to follow up proposal asking for $100,000 gift for a room in the fine arts center	$100,000

7. Allocate sufficient resources for the development function.

"Be overly generous in budget; be lean and mean in evaluation. With adequate funding, your development office should measure up well in a lean-and-mean evaluation, and should justify the good judgment you show by investing in it" (Evans, 1989, page 146).

In the academic world where tight budgets are a constant reality, allocating sufficient funds to the development function is extremely difficult. Presidents frequently ask: "How can I adequately budget for the fundraising process in light of competing alternatives?" Fisher recommends that a president "approve a budgetary allocation that is more than you are initially inclined to grant" (1989, page 11). He notes that an investment in fundraising will pay rich rewards over time in increased gifts to the institution. Similarly, Lewis urges nonprofit organizations to invest more money in fundraising: "Increasing giving at a faster rate of growth will require a wise investment in fund raising at a faster rate" (1991, page 257).

In considering budgets, it is recommended that sufficient resources be made available to provide operating funds for travel, conferences, support personnel, brochures, and other materials. All too often, a significant investment is made in personnel, but inadequate support resources are provided. This creates a scenario in which development personnel are appropriately paid but do not have the funds to travel, meet with donors, buy needed computer hardware and software, and produce brochures to tell the institutional story.

What constitutes a wise investment in fundraising for the small college? In a study of effective fundraising institutions, Loessin, Duronio, and Barton found that the amount of money spent on fundraising programs is an important variable for predicting total voluntary support. Their data suggest that, in general, the more money spent on fundraising programs, the more money raised (1987).

A 1991 survey of CIC colleges found that independent colleges invest significant resources in fundraising efforts. Institutions of all sizes invest an average of $295,990 in fundraising salaries, benefits, travel, media/promotion, and other costs (Dowden, 1993, page 31).

Are these expenditures enough? How do the small colleges in the survey compare to other higher education institutions? How much should it cost to raise a dollar? **Expenditures in Fund Raising, Alumni Relations, and Other Constituent (Public) Relations** [a study of 51 colleges and universities, conducted by the Council for Advancement and Support of Education (CASE) and the National Association of College and University Business Officers (NACUBO) and funded by the Lilly Endowment, Inc.] confirms "the conventional wisdom that fundraising costs in the aggregate usually run about 15 percent of the amount raised" (1990, page 12). It also notes that many other factors affect the cost of raising a dollar and direct comparisons from one institution to another are somewhat difficult. However this CASE/NACUBO research revealed the following cost benchmarks:

- It costs between eight and 16 cents to raise one dollar.
- The return on investment of dollars spent in fundraising programs ranges from 525 percent to 1,150 percent.
- The average institution spends just over 2 percent of its total educational and general budget for fundraising.
- The amount spent on fundraising per student enrolled ranges from $67 to $379.
- The amount spent on fundraising per alumnus of record ranges from $20 to $47.
- Each fundraising professional accounts for an average of $500,000 to $1.1 million in gift revenue produced.
- "The amounts generated by the college or university development program exceed the salaries paid to development personnel (including support staff) by a factor of ten or more."

- Fundraising personnel expenditures range from 58.1 percent to 68.5 percent of total fundraising costs.

- Services, supplies, and other expenditures for fundraising range from 31.5 percent to 41.9 percent of total fundraising costs (1990, pages 17-29).

The other side of the budgetary coin is effective evaluation. Once development offices have been given adequate budgets, they must be held accountable for meeting fundraising goals. All too often development officers argue that development budgets must be increased so that specific fundraising goals can be met. The president is inclined to grant such a request, fearing dire consequences if goals are not achieved. Unfortunately, the college president often does not follow up the request by monitoring the progress of the development office and holding it accountable to meeting the goals. Adequate funding must be accompanied by accountability (Fisher, 1989, pages 11-16).

Slinker found that college presidents hold development staffs accountable by reviewing goals and objectives and tracking progress. Of the surveyed presidents, 15 percent reviewed long-range fundraising goals and objectives with development staffs at least monthly, with 37 percent performing such a review biannually, and 44 percent annually (1988, page 102). Once the goals are set, he found that presidents frequently track progress in meeting the goals. Thirty-three percent of the presidents indicated they track fundraising progress weekly and 56 percent track it monthly (1988, page 105).

A dollar spent in development can be a wise investment if accompanied by specific fundraising goals and accountability for them. An effective college president sees to it that these two areas are tightly linked.

8. Seek out educational opportunities in fundraising.

> "Fund raising will become an increasingly important role for all college presidents, regardless of size, funding, or mission. One might as well learn to be good at it" (The Role of the President in Fund Raising, pages 3, 4).

To be effective in fundraising, presidents should consider keeping current with the literature in the field of philanthropy and attending periodic workshops and seminars designed to inform, update, and motivate regarding the fundraising process. Felicetti describes this presidential role as one of "being a work study student." He comments that "it should be no cause for embarrassment that the heads of small colleges are in perpetual need of on-the-job training when much of their advancement work must be done without the insulation of a large university staff" (1993, page 65). Educational needs are different from president to president, depending on interests and career paths.

Although more and more presidents are being selected from the ranks of experienced fund raisers, (McMillen, 1991, page A35-36) the most typical route to college presidency is through the academic side of higher education. The 1989 study indicated that this was true for Coalition presidents as well. "Academic administrator" was the most frequently cited position held just prior to assuming the presidency.

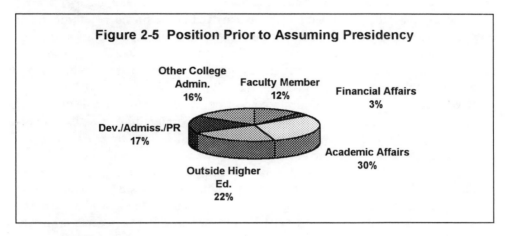

Figure 2-5 Position Prior to Assuming Presidency

Further, Coalition presidents listed "academic administrator" and "faculty member" most frequently when asked to name the positions they held during their careers in higher education. (See Figures 2-5 and 2-6). Similar results were discovered in the 1991 survey of Council of Independent Colleges members. Only 12 percent of the CIC respondents indicated that the president had held a development or advancement position immediately prior to assuming the presidency. In contrast, 40 percent had been academic administrators, and 5 percent had been faculty members (Felicetti, 1993, page 65).

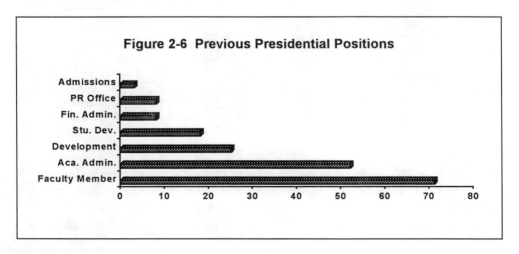

Figure 2-6 Previous Presidential Positions

41

It is clear from this data that "academic administration" and "faculty service" are the predominant paths to the Christian college presidency. A majority of presidents come to their positions with limited or no professional experience in fundraising, public relations, or admissions. Fisher and Quehl note that this problem is universal to higher education. "Institutional advancement . . . is perhaps most frequently the area with which newly appointed college and university presidents are least familiar. Yet it is this area, more than any other, that will determine the extent to which [a presidency] is deemed worthy or unworthy" (1989, page 4).

Fisher comments: "Presidents who have arrived at the presidency through the academic chairs are especially prone to shun their external responsibilities. Indeed, many presidents of this type never quite make it onto the presidential platform because they are unable to draw sufficiently far away from their academic background where they are more comfortable" (1984, page 122).

Even though Coalition presidents come from predominantly academic backgrounds, they describe their fundraising skills as generally above average. Sixty-two percent, in the 1989 study, indicated that their skills were strong or above average, while 38 percent indicated that their skills were average or below.

Research indicates that most presidents learn their fundraising skills through on-the-job training. Cook, in his 1994 study, found that "presidents acquire their fund raising knowledge and training primarily through on-the-job administrative experience" (1994, page 3). The 1991 CIC survey found that presidents primarily acquired their fundraising skills through practical experience. Likewise, Coalition presidents also indicated, in the 1989 study, that their fundraising skills were largely learned through trial and error and at conferences. (See Figure 2-7.)

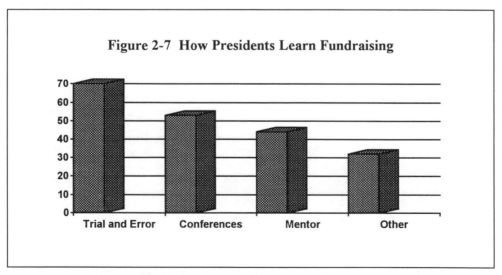

Figure 2-7 How Presidents Learn Fundraising

In spite of the fact that Coalition presidents felt that they have above average skills in fundraising, most desired additional educational opportunities in fundraising. Seventy percent indicated that they agree, or strongly agree, that such opportunities would be helpful. Consider the following educational opportunities recommended by Coalition presidents in the 1989 study:

- **Spend time with other presidents.**

   Effective college presidents take sufficient time to talk with one another about their struggles and frustrations, joys and successes in fundraising. These times can be therapeutic and helpful, according to the assessment of Coalition presidents who participated in the presidents' study. One commented: "I have lived in this world [of Christian colleges] for some years and have never before heard that there are other people struggling with these issues."

   Coalition presidents enthusiastically endorsed the concept of "presidents only" workshops or conferences to allow them to share fundraising experiences. One president commented: "We need an opportunity for discussion with each other without experts. We don't need more slick techniques and gimmicks. We need people who know what's going on in higher education and will share it with people who care." One president who had participated in such "presidential sharing" sessions noted: "I learned more from listening to other presidents than from all the CASE conferences I have been to." Another commented: "I would like to listen to other presidents, share ideas, and swap war stories." Fisher, Tack, and Wheeler also recommend such a method for training college presidents. "By reading and discussing specific cases in an open forum, [presidents] can see the complexity of issues and are encouraged to weigh the pros and cons of possible problem-solving strategies" (1988, page 95).

   Coalition presidents noted that "presidents only" workshops should focus on both general and specialized topics. Most frequently cited were workshops on major donor identification/cultivation/solicitation, planned giving, proposal writing, fundraising planning, foundation and corporation fundraising, and public relations.

- **Attend workshops with institutional teams.**

   Effective presidents seek out opportunities to attend conferences with institutional colleagues, including trustees and fundraising staff. Sixty-five percent of the Coalition presidents indicated that attending a workshop with an institutional team, including presidents, development staff, and trustees, would be the most effective fundraising training method available. The Council for the Advancement and Support of Education (CASE) and several other organizations hold such conferences. Conference benefits go far beyond the information imparted. Time together as an institutional team promotes communication, camaraderie, and understanding. In many instances, this is the first opportunity for open communication to take place between these three diverse groups.

   If a suitable conference cannot be found, perhaps an institutional team could meet on campus with an outside facilitator or could interact with a team from a nearby sister institution. Such methods will yield rich benefits by opening channels of communication among trustees, presidents, and development staffs.

- **Develop mentor relationships.**

    In a survey of college presidents, Fisher, Tack, and Wheeler discovered that presidents favored "internships or master-apprentice relationships" as a method of training a president (1988, page 96). One quarter of the Coalition presidents also cited this method as helpful. The process of finding a colleague and developing a close mentor/mentee relationship can bring significant rewards to both parties. The mentee can learn from a more experienced president the pitfalls and strategies of fundraising, while the mentor can develop new insights into fundraising problems and issues for application to his or her own campus situations. For both mentor and mentee, the relationship can produce fellowship and friendship and allow an opportunity to share frustrations that typically cannot be shared with campus colleagues. Both parties will be enriched by a mentor/mentee relationship.

- **Develop consultant relationships.**

    Hiring a consultant is often a difficult, controversial decision on a Christian college campus. While trustees understand the importance of hiring outside personnel to design buildings and to audit budgets, they often do not understand the need to spend money for fundraising consultation. One frequently heard comment is: "That's why we hired good development officers. We assumed they were the experts and we would not need other outside assistance."

    Despite the often difficult process of hiring a fundraising consultant, the benefits can be great. Fundraising consultants bring with them a wealth of experiences and ideas learned from working with other institutions. They offer a fresh perspective not tied to institutional personalities or politics. They often can help the president see through the morass of past experience and recommend effective courses of action.

    Many professional fundraising consultants do not come cheap. Often their daily fees exceed the monthly salary of some of the institution's development officers. However, less expensive options can be secured. For example, presidents often hire working development officers from sister institutions. Names of successful professionals can be obtained from the Council for the Advancement and Support of Education and from the Coalition for Christian Colleges & Universities. Whether part-time or full-time consultants are secured, if they are selected carefully and with a view toward institutional fit, they can pay their way many times over in increased revenue to the institution.

    It is recommended that consultants be hired by the president of the institution and not by the development office, so they can be objective in their evaluation of development personnel. Further, development consultants should be selected on the basis of the expertise they bring to the assignment and their fit with the institution. A determination should be made regarding in what areas the consultant will work, then a consultant should be sought with expertise in the necessary fields. An attempt should also be made to find a consultant who understands the evangelical Christian college. This understanding is important to the consultant's working effectively with the board, major donors, and other volunteers.

- **Review fundraising literature.**

    Effective presidential leaders in fundraising keep current with literature in the field. Numerous publications are available through the Association of Governing Boards (AGB), the Council for the Advancement and Support of Education (CASE), the American Council on Education (ACE), and the Christian Stewardship Association (CSA). Several periodicals, including **The Chronicle of Philanthropy** and **CASE Currents,** offer updated information on ideas and issues in the fundraising world. Many presidents make it a practice to read such publications to apprise themselves of the latest issues in fundraising and the proper questions to ask of a development staff. One helpful book is Fisher and Quehl's 1989 work **The President and Fund Raising**, an outstanding handbook for both new and experienced presidents

- **Seek educational opportunities that focus on biblical perspectives.**

    For Christians in fundraising, particular attention should be given to finding educational opportunities which present biblical perspectives on fundraising. Coalition presidents expressed a strong desire to participate in such experiences. In particular, they emphasized the need to discuss the concept of stewardship and servanthood. Many felt there was an advantage to Christian-oriented educational opportunities in fundraising. One commented: "We are in this together." Another stated: "We face ethical dilemmas that are not even thought about at state schools." One book of particular help in wrestling with the question of biblical guidelines to fundraising is Wesley K. Willmer's **Money for Ministries** (1989).

9. Consider, discuss, and encourage integration of Christian faith and fundraising practices.

> "It is a difficult task to think and act like Christians in the business of raising money for God's work....Christian fund raisers know the bottom-line reality, that while a ministry must be baptized in prayer, it is fueled by money. Finding a godly standard by which to do both is not easy" (Lockerbie, 1989, page 199).

A diversity of viewpoints is expressed by Coalition presidents when discussing Christian perspectives in fundraising. The 1989 survey found that most indicated a desire to discuss these issues with colleagues. One commented: "We should come together to talk about the unique aspects of fund raising for Christian schools to plow some new ground."

It is clear that effective presidents at Coalition institutions take time to consider, discuss, and encourage the integration of scriptural principles with fundraising practices. This process will be different for each college based on theological persuasions and denominational backgrounds. However, the very process of thinking about and questioning whether a college's fundraising methods are scriptural helps focus attention on the Word as the foundation for fundraising actions. In other words, the inquiry is as important as the outcome. The inquiry process tends to change the attitudes of the participants and directs thoughts and energies toward the question: "Is my institution raising funds in a Christian manner?"

Each institution will develop a different set of answers to this question. The diversity of opinion among Christian colleges was seen in response to the 1989 survey question, "Are proven fund raising techniques in tension with scriptural principles?" Coalition presidents were asked whether techniques such as gift clubs, signature machines, premiums, donor recognition, and donor research are appropriate for use by Christians. A majority of the presidents did not see a tension between these techniques and scriptural principles. The feeling was that "we use these techniques as long as the basic mission and purpose of the college is the foundation for all we do in fund raising."

A number of Coalition presidents, however, were clearly bothered by conflicts between "proven techniques" and Christian principles. Yet they use these techniques in their fundraising programs. One commented: "If we don't use the techniques that are used by others, we are going to get kicked around by the competition." Another acknowledged that he does not feel good about using these proven fundraising techniques and "feels like a prostitute" when doing so.

In contrast, some presidents did have a concern about several of the proven fundraising techniques and viewed them as "unchristian." Most typically cited were gift clubs, computerized letters, signature machines, and premiums. Coalition presidents' comments regarding scriptural principles as compared with proven fundraising techniques demonstrate the wide diversity of theological thought within the evangelical world and highlight the need for discussion on these issues. However, it is clear that the effective college president sets an example by considering the questions of integration of faith and practice whenever fundraising plans, policies, procedures, and techniques are discussed.

10. Demonstrate integrity in fundraising tasks.

> "We are facing an integrity crisis. Not only is the conduct of the church in question, but so is the very character of the church" (Wiersbe, 1988, page 17).

David Le Shana, president of Western Evangelical Seminary, commented at the 1990 Christian College Coalition annual meeting: "Fund raising needs to be marked by integrity and measured by ministry." These are important words in an era that has seen the integrity of the Christian fund raiser plummet to new lows as Christian leaders are exposed for financial and fundraising improprieties. A survey by The Non-Profit Times/Opinion Research Corporation indicated that less than

40 percent of the American public felt fund raisers were highly trustworthy. The good news is that fund raisers were considered more trustworthy than lawyers, politicians, or stock-brokers (**The Non-Profit Times**, March 1990, page 17).

Hopefully, more than 40 percent of Christian college constituents view institutional fundraising efforts as highly trustworthy. Christian college fund raisers should help to ensure that institutions gain and deserve the trust of constituents by maintaining integrity in all fundraising endeavors. Fundraising needs to be marked by honesty, trustworthiness, and openness.

Coalition presidents sense deeply this unique responsibility inherent in planning fundraising campaigns and projects for Christian institutions. The presidents, in the 1989 study, suggested that Christian colleges need to articulate the Christian mission with honesty, integrity, and stewardship accountability. One suggested: "We have to judge the methods we use by our values. Is it honest and truthful, rather than by the world's way?" As a result of these special responsibilities, many felt that there is a difference between fundraising methods at a Christian school versus a secular school. One president responded: "We ask people to give to the Kingdom; therefore, fund raising activities will be different." Another said: "There is a tension in the way we recognize wealthy people over the smaller donor. Our methods need to be squeaky clean." Another stated: "It is stewardship that our donors give to."

Not only do effective presidents develop a fundraising program "marked by integrity," but one that is "measured by ministry." Gordon K. Moyes comments: "Responsible giving or stewardship is not man's way of raising money, but God's way of raising people" (1989, page 33). Fundraising is a ministry. Christian fund raisers minister to a person's need, present an opportunity for an investment in the Kingdom, and help him or her to grow to further service to the church and to Christ.

A dentist, commenting on the fundraising process, said: "So, you're going out to extract some money from people." To which came the reply: "No, John, you do the extractions, I encourage people to invest in the Kingdom." A subtle difference maybe, but an important one. In ministering to people, Christian fund raisers do not manipulate them into giving money, but encourage them in their own Christian growth through their investment in the work of the Kingdom.

An important principle in Scripture is highlighted in II Corinthians 8:5, "... they gave themselves first to the Lord and then to us in keeping with God's will" (NIV). Paul commends those in the church at Corinth for first committing themselves to the Lord and then giving of their resources to support Paul's work. This two-step process is important and significant. In a fundraising ministry, one is encouraging people to give themselves to the Lord through the giving of their resources. What a wonderful task Christian college presidents are called to fulfill for the Kingdom. Effective presidential leadership in fundraising is characterized by integrity and a call to ministry.

The Joys of Leadership

Effective presidential leadership is important to the success of any higher education institution. The president must exert this leadership in order to be effective in his or her institution. Work in fundraising does not keep the president from exerting institutional leadership, but helps him or her to exercise leadership by encouraging others to see the vision and plans for the future and to invest in them.

Fundraising for a Christian college president is a godly task. Money is raised for a vital and compelling mission: to educate men and women as scholar-servants in order to meet the needs of a diverse and changing world. What a significant calling!

And in all of it, one should find joy in the process of encouraging others to invest in the great ministry of the evangelical liberal arts college. Fisher writes: "There are few feelings more exhilarating than in bringing in the big gift" (1984, page 167). For the Christian, exhilaration should result not from a feeling of having brought home the "big one", but from the joy in knowing that one of God's children has been encouraged to further invest in the Kingdom. One can see this joy in the face of the donor, and it is reflected in the fundraiser's countenance as well. Go out and enjoy this great experience that the Lord has given.

RESOURCES

Adams, Michael F. "Teamwork at the Top: The Development Officer's View." **Currents**, July/August 1989.

Anderson, Wayne. "Presidents Must Make Fund Raising Work." **AGB Reports**, November/December 1984.

Augsburger, Myron. From letter, June 30, 1994.

Bishop, Lawrence A. and Hurtubise, Mark. "Who Are Successful Fund-raising Presidents?" **AGB Reports**, March/April 1991.

Boardman, William H. "An Effective Model of a Principal Gift Program." **Developing an Effective Major Gift Program: From Managing Staff to Soliciting Gifts**. Ed. by Roy Muir and Jerry May. Washington DC: Council for Advancement and Support of Education, 1993.

Breneman, David W. "Higher Education: On a Collision Course with New Realities." **American Student Assistance**, December 1993.

Broce, Thomas E. "Setting the PACE: The ROLE of Governing Boards in Fund Raising." Date unknown.

Brown, Robert W. "The Presidential Role in Financial Development." **Courage in Mission: Presidential Leadership in the Church-related College**. Ed. by Duane H. Dagley. Washington, DC: Council for Advancement and Support of Education, 1988.

"Colleges and Universities Should Place High Priority on Obtaining Major Gifts from Individuals." **Bulletin on Public Relations and Development**. Naperville, IL: Gonser Gerber Tinker Stuhr, September, 1993.

Cook, Weaver Bruce. **Courting Philanthropy: The Role of University Presidents and Chancellors in Fund Raising** (abstract). Ann Arbor: University Microfilms, 1994.

Cosovich, Joe. "An Introduction to the Major Gift Process." **Developing an Effective Major Gift Program: From Managing Staff to Soliciting Gifts.** Ed. by Roy Muir and Jerry May. Washington DC: Council for Advancement and Support of Education, 1993.

Costello, Kathryn R. "What I Expect of my CEO." **Currents**, November/December 1993.

Dailey, William F. "Organizing Yourself for Major Gift Success." **The Successful Capital Campaign.** Ed. by H. Gerald Quigg. Washington, DC: Council for Advancement and Support of Education, 1986.

Dingman, Robert W. **Recruiting the Right Development Officer Seminar**. Washington, DC: Christian College Coalition, January 30, 1995.

Dorich, Dina. "The Making of a President." **Currents**, April 1991.

Dowden, G. Blair. "Development: Winning Strategies for Fund-raising Success." **Winning Strategies in Challenging Times for Advancing Small Colleges.** Ed. by Wesley K. Willmer. Washington, DC: Council for the Advancement and Support of Education, 1993.

Dowden, G. Blair: "Presidents: Effective Fund Raising Leadership." **Friends, Funds, and Freshmen: A Manager's Guide to Christian College Advancement.** Ed. by Wesley K. Willmer. Washington, DC: Christian College Coalition, 1990.

Dyson, Dave, and Kirkman, Ralph. "Presidential Priorities." **AGB Reports,** March /April 1989.

Edwards, Norman L. "Fund Raising Workshop." Huntington College Board of Trustees' Retreat, January 1993.

Evans, Gary A. "Financing the Development Program." **The President and Fund Raising.** Ed. by James L. Fisher and Gary H. Quehl. San Francisco: Jossey-Bass Inc., 1989.

Expenditures in Fund Raising, Alumni Relations and other Constituent (Public) Relations. Washington, DC: Council for Advancement and Support of Education, 1990.

Felicetti, Daniel A. "The Advancement Roles of Small College Presidents." **Winning Strategies in Challenging Times for Advancing Small Colleges.** Ed. by Wesley K. Willmer. Washington, DC.: Council for the Advancement and Support of Education, 1993.

Fisher, James L. "A History of Philanthropy." **The President and Fund Raising.** Ed. by James L. Fisher and Gary H. Quehl. San Francisco: Jossey-Bass Inc., 1989.

Fisher, James L. "Establishing a Successful Fund-Raising Program." **The President and Fund Raising.** Ed. by James L. Fisher and Gary H. Quehl. San Francisco: Jossey-Bass Inc., 1989.

Fisher, James L. **Power of the Presidency.** New York: Macmillan Publishing Company, 1984.

Fisher, James L. and Quehl, Gary H., Ed. **The President and Fund Raising.** San Francisco: Jossey-Bass Inc., 1989.

Fisher, James L., Tack, Martha W., and Wheeler, Karen J. **The Effective College President.** New York: Macmillan Publishing Company, 1988.

Fisher, Mark A. "Seasoned CEO's." **Currents**, November/December 1993.

Gale, Robert L. "The Role of the Governing Board." **The President and Fund Raising.** Ed. by James L. Fisher and Gary H. Quehl. New York: Macmillan Publishing Company, 1989.

Hamlin, Alan. "The President as Salesman." **Educational Record**, Winter 1990.

Hamlin, Alan and Hungerford, Curtiss. "How Private Colleges Survive Financial Crisis." **AGB Reports**, May/June 1989.

Hurtubise, Mark. **An Analysis of Presidential Attitudes Toward and Participation in Fund Raising at Select, Small, Independent, Liberal Arts Colleges and Universities**. Ann Arbor: University Microfilms, 1988.

"In College Fundraising, President's Role Is Found More Important Than Planning." **The Chronicle of Philanthropy,** July 25, 1989.

Janney, Scott R.P. **The College President and Fund Raising Effectiveness** (abstract). Ann Arbor: University Microfilms, 1994.

Keeping the Chief Development Officer that You Recruit Seminar. Washington, DC: Christian College Coalition, January 30, 1995.

Kesler, Jay L. Comments presented at 1990 annual meeting, Christian College Coalition, Washington, DC, January 1990.

Le Shana, David C. "Building a Team in a Christian College." **Courage in Mission: Presidential Leadership in the Church-related College.** Ed. by Duane H. Dagley. Washington, DC: Council for Advancement and Support of Education, 1988.

Le Shana, David C. Comments presented at 1990 annual meeting, Christian College Coalition, Washington, DC, January 1990.

Lewis, Wilson C. "Investing More Money in Fund Raising—Wisely." **Taking Fund Raising Seriously**. Ed. by Dwight F. Burlingame and Lamar and J. Hulse. San Francisco: Jossey-Bass Inc, 1991.

Lockerbie, D. Bruce. "Preserving the Person in the Fund-Raising Process." **Money for Ministries.** Ed. by Wesley K. Willmer. Wheaton, IL: Victor Books, 1989.

Loessin, Bruce A. and Duronio, Margaret A. "The Role of Planning in Successful Fund Raising in Ten Higher Education Institutions." Paper presented at annual conference, Society for College and University Planning, Denver, CO, July 1989.

Loessin, Bruce A., Duronio, Margaret A., and Barton, Georgina L. "Fund Raising Effectiveness in Higher Education." Unpublished study, University of Pittsburgh, 1987.

Lorentzen, Melvin E. "Does It Pay To Pray?" **Money for Ministries.** Ed. by Wesley K. Willmer. Wheaton, IL: Victor Books, 1989.

MacMillan, David F. "Development: Building a Balanced Program." **Friends, Funds, and Freshmen: A Manager's Guide to Christian College Advancement**. Ed. by Wesley K. Willmer. Washington, DC: Christian College Coalition, 1990.

McMillen, Liz. "More Colleges Top Fund Raisers for Presidencies, Seeking Expertise in Strategic Thinking About Entire Institution." **The Chronicle of Higher Education**, September 11, 1991.

Moisan, Leonard J. "Because That's Where the Money Is." **AGB Reports**, September/October 1992.

Mooney, Carolyn J. "Study Examines Turnover Rates in 12 Campus Jobs." **The Chronicle of Higher Education**, February 10, 1993.

Moore, H. Martin. "A Model of Cooperation." **Currents**, July/August 1987.

Moyes, Gordon K. "God's Call For Responsible Giving." **Money for Ministries.** Ed. by Wesley K. Willmer. Wheaton, IL: Victor Books, 1989.

Mullet, Steven. "The Definition and Philosophy of Institutional Advancement." **Handbook of Institutional Advancement.** Ed. by A. Wesley Rowland. San Francisco: Jossey-Bass Inc., 1977.

Nanus, Burt. **Visionary Leadership**. San Francisco: Jossey-Bass, Inc., 1992.

Neff, Robert W. "The Trustees' Critical Role in Small College Advancement." **Winning Strategies in Challenging Times for Advancing Small Colleges.** Ed. by Wesley K. Willmer. Washington, DC: Council for the Advancement and Support of Education, 1993.

Nelson, Jeffrey B. "Planning:" Establishing Program Goals and Strategies." **Handbook of Institutional Advancement**. Ed. by A. Wesley Rowland. San Francisco: Jossey-Bass Inc., 1977.

Ness, Frederic W. **The President's Role in Development**. Washington, DC: Association of American Colleges, 1975.

Non Profit Times, The. "Less Than Half of Americans Rate Fundraisers Trustworthy." March 1990.

Recruiting the Right Development Officer Seminar. Washington, DC: Christian College Coalition, January 30, 1995.

Rodriguez, Charles G. **Alumni and the President: Presidential Leadership Behavior Affecting Alumni Giving at Small Private Liberal Arts Colleges.** Ann Arbor: University Microfilms, 1991.

Rowland, A. Westley, Ed. **Handbook of Institutional Advancement.** San Francisco: Jossey-Bass Inc., 1977.

Rowland, A. Westley. "Perspectives on Institutional Advancement." **Handbook of Institutional Advancement.** Ed. by A. Wesley Rowland. San Francisco: Jossey-Bass Inc., 1977.

Sammartino, Peter. **The President of a Small College.** New York: Cornwall Books, 1982.

Shea, James M. "Organization and Structure." **Handbook of Institutional Advancement.** Ed. by A. Wesley Rowland. San Francisco: Jossey-Bass Inc., 1977.

Slinker, John Michael. **The Role of the College or University President in Institutional Advancement.** Ann Arbor: University Microfilms, 1988.

Smith, G. T. "The Development Program." **Handbook of Institutional Advancement**. 1st ed. (1977), quoted in David R. Dunlop - "Special Concerns of Major Gift Fund-Raising." **Handbook of Institutional Advancement** (2nd ed.). Ed. by A. Westley Rowland. San Francisco: Jossey-Bass, 1986.

Stachitas, Martha. **Recruiting the Right Development Officer Seminar**. Washington, DC: Christian College Coalition, January 30, 1995.

"The Role of the President in Fund Raising." Paper presented for Council for Advancement and Support of Education Workshop. Author and date unknown.

Trachtenberg, Stephen Joel. "What I Expect of My CDO." **Currents**, November/December 1993.

Vaccaro, Louis C. "The President and Planning: Management and Vision." **Courage in Mission: Presidential Leadership in the Church-related College.** Ed. by Duane H. Dagley. Washington, DC: Council for Advancement and Support of Education, 1988.

"The Role of the President in Fund Raising." Paper presented for Council for Advancement and Support of Education Workshop. Author and date unknown.

Wesley, John. **The Works of John Wesley.** Volume 3, Ed. by Albert C. Outler. Nashville: Abingdon Press, 1986.

West, Dan C. "The Presidency of a Small College." **Management Techniques for Small and Specialized Institutions.** Ed. by Andrew J. Falander and John C. Merson. San Francisco: Jossey-Bass Inc., 1983.

Wiersbe, Warren W. **The Integrity Crisis.** Nashville: Oliver-Nelson Books, 1988.

Wiggins, Norman W. "Selection and Involvement of Trustees Key to Successful Development Program." **Bulletin on Public Relations and Development.** Naperville, IL: Gonser Gerber Tinker Stuhr, January, 1988.

Willmer, Wesley K. **A New Look at Managing the Small College Advancement Program.** Washington, DC: Council for Advancement and Support of Education, 1987.

Willmer, Wesley K., Ed. **Friends, Funds, and Freshmen: A Manager's Guide to Christian College Advancement.** Washington, DC: Christian College Coalition, 1990.

Willmer, Wesley K., Ed. **Money for Ministries.** Wheaton, IL: Victor Books, 1989.

Willmer, Wesley K., Ed. **Winning Strategies in Challenging Times for Advancing Small Colleges.** Washington, DC: Council for the Advancement and Support of Education, 1993.

About the Author

G. BLAIR DOWDEN serves as president of Huntington College in Huntington, Indiana, where he has been actively involved in fundraising and friend raising. Prior to his service at Huntington College, he spent seven years as vice president for development at Houghton College in Houghton, NY, where he directed a successful $13.5 million capital campaign.

*He also has served in several administrative posts at Taylor University, in Upland, Indiana, including special assistant to the president. He has authored several articles, including "Presidents: Effective Fund-Raising Leadership," which appeared in the 1990 book, **Friends, Funds, and Freshmen: A Manager's Guide to Christian College Advancement**, and "Development: Winning Strategies for Fund Raising Success," which appeared in **Winning Strategies in Challenging Times for Advancing Small Colleges** (1993). His guide to alumni involvement in admissions has been widely circulated among small liberal arts colleges.*

He has served on several boards in the fundraising area, including the National Advisory Board for the Christian College Coalition Lilly Fund-Raising Project, Christian Stewardship Association, and the Independent Colleges of Indiana Foundation.

A consultant and conference speaker on fundraising and higher education issues, Dowden holds a B.A. from Wheaton College (Illinois) and an M.A. and Ed.D. from Ball State University. He and his wife, Chris, have two children, Beau and Marli.

Chapter 3

Development through the Eyes of Faith

ADAM J. MORRIS

Development is a high pressure job! The goals are always rising, deadlines are short, and once one project is complete, 10 more are right there waiting. It seems as if the work is never done. At Christian colleges and universities, the daily pressures of having to balance the budget, increase scholarship support, provide for capital expansion, and build the endowment are omnipresent. These efforts are vital to the fiscal health of the institutions, have very tangible outcomes, and are often monitored closely by the board of trustees.

With these pressures comes the challenge of finding enough waking hours in the day to fully accomplish all of these concerns. Unfortunately, the natural tendency is to seek every workable method available to raise more money. Is it possible, in this pressured climate, that some of our techniques have actually taken us outside the parameters of acceptable fundraising principles provided in Scripture?

In a speech entitled, "What's So Christian About Our Fund Raising," Dr. R. Scott Rodin, vice president for advancement at Eastern Baptist Theological Seminary, discussed how Christian colleges and universities often model their development efforts after sucessful secular models like Harvard, Stanford, and Ohio State (1995). Rodin claims there is an overwhelming tendency among Christian institutions to "'Christianize' fundraising techniques to make them more acceptable to our donors and more palatable to our boards." He states examples such as "Bible verses inserted into otherwise secular appeal letters, the use of premiums of a religious nature but with the same goal as the state college's football regalia or school logo merchandise, and the ever present request for 'financial *and prayer* support.'"

Dian Little expressed similar concerns in a speech to Christian development officers and asked them two very pointed questions:

- Can you give me the location in Scripture of the imperatives which drive your fundraising efforts?
- Can you relate the Scriptural guidelines you use in dealing with donors?

Little's conclusion was quite simple: "Secular techniques and methodology determine our work model rather than scriptural imperatives" (1995).

Rodin and Little are not saying that all techniques and programs used by secular institutions and modeled by Christian colleges and universities are inherently wrong. Rather, they are challenging Christian colleges and universities to look at their development program from a biblical perspective and in Rodin's words, "only incorporate those techniques which are a clear and honest fit."

There are hundreds of "how to" guides available on the market today that can show the Christian development officer how to raise money. This chapter attempts to come along side and complement those resources by providing some relevant, practical insight into how biblical principles can and should be integrated into the daily operations of the development office. What does it mean to raise money *through the eyes of faith*? How does a development office model a biblical approach to budgeting, staffing, and strategizing, and to the cultivation, solicitation, and long-term relationships we have with our donors? In the following pages an attempt will be made to answer these questions by looking at six areas within the development function. They are:

- Key principles of biblical stewardship
- Managing institutional resources
- Equipping of staff
- The role of the chief development officer
- Cultivating the heart of the donor
- The donor's response

Four Key Principles of Biblical Stewardship

Stewardship is a term with which many are familiar, but few can clearly define. Two respected voices on biblical stewardship, Ronald Vallet and Wesley Willmer, have provided helpful biblical definitions of stewardship. Vallet states, "Stewardship is nothing less than a complete lifestyle, a total accountability and responsibility before God. Stewardship is what we do after we say we believe, that is, after we give our love, loyalty and trust to God, from whom each and every aspect of our lives comes as a gift" (1989, page 4). Willmer adds that "stewardship is a way of looking at life and, more importantly, a way of living Christ-like in a non-Christian world. Stewardship is God's way of raising people—not man's way of raising money" (1994, page 4).

With these definitions as the foundation upon which our development efforts should be built, I have found four key stewardship principles from Scripture helpful in keeping the day-to-day pressures of the job in perspective.

1. Acknowledge that God is the source of all of our resources. Psalm 24:1 tells us that God owns everything, and He is the provider of everything we have.

2. As the book of Genesis reminds us, humankind is made in the image of God. People are valued and are important to God for who they are, not just for their resources.

3. Because our work is God's work, He supports us in our enterprise. Exodus 25:2 reminds us that God has provided all that is necessary to accomplish His work.

4. Remember that we are "workers in His vineyard"—we are His instruments to accomplish His purposes. Zechariah 4:6 tells us, " 'Not by might nor by power, but by my spirit,' says the Lord Almighty."

Managing Institutional Resources

The book of James states that "every good thing bestowed and every perfect gift is from above." At our Christian institutions, these "good things" and "perfect gifts" can take on many forms. Whether it's an increased enrollment, a new building, or the gifts an institution receives, God's blessings are widely evident. But His provisions are not without certain expectations. Such provisions carry with them tremendous responsibility to be good stewards. In fact, Matthew 25 shows us that God's *continued* provision is directly linked to faithful stewardship.

In the development office of a Christian college or university, one of our greatest stewardship responsibilities is how we manage the resources required to meet our demanding goals. Our ultimate responsibility is to God, but we must also be sensitive to the messages our actions send to donors. From the quality of premiums being sent to the types of events being held, the actions of the development office can often communicate a strong message of institutional stewardship. It is easy to forget how closely our donors watch our activities.

The key is finding a balance and spending only what is required to get the job done. David Hubbard, in a booklet for Christian development officers, reminds us that we need to be able to justify what we spend in terms of the "direct function it plays within the mission of the institution" (1994). Hubbard reminds us that the resources we manage are God's!

With this as a Scriptural foundation, there is a practical side to examine as well. One of the "10 basic laws or principles" of fundraising according to Harold J. Seymore in the 1950s is "you can't raise money without spending money; within reasonable limits the return is likely to be commensurate with the investment" (1960, page 5).

In 1994, the Coalition for Christian Colleges & Universities (CCCU), with funding from the Lilly Endowment, Inc., distributed a Resource Development Survey to all its member institutions. The survey was the third such instrument sent to chief development officers since 1985 with the purpose of exploring trends related to institutional advancement at Christian colleges and universities. The surveys asked numerous questions related to the field of development and the responses have been incorporated into the pages that follow.

One survey question explored the area of institutional expenditures with a question designed to reveal all costs related to fundraising. As Table 3-1 shows, the mean fundraising expenditures increased 19 percent between 1989 and 1994, from $253,272 to $311,103. An even greater increase occurs when comparing 1985 mean figures to those in 1994. Note the increases from 1985 to 1994 in the 501-750, 1001-1250, and 1501-2000 enrollment categories. It is fair to say that the development function has "come of age" at member institutions of all sizes.

Table 3-1
Fundraising Expenditures:
(Including Salaries and Benefits, Travel, Media/Promotion, etc.)
by Enrollment Size

Enrollment	1994 High	1994 Low	1994 Mean	1989 Mean	1985 Mean
Up to 500	$313,243	$55,000	$167,150	$116,562	$159,536
501-750	324,584	85,580	209,811	188,567	94,000
751-1000	593,386	115,000	249,036	199,069	192,951
1001-1250	632,776	118,388	349,382	312,934	127,560
1251-1500	527,000	140,000	295,280	279,073	362,070
1501-2000	874,358	90,000	413,728	420,270	212,277
2001+	1,458,041	324,045	696,168	447,454	605,450
Survey Mean of All Groups			311,103	253,372	

Wilson C. Lewis urges nonprofit organizations to invest more money in fundraising and states that "increasing giving at a faster rate of growth will require wise investment in fundraising at a faster rate" (1991, page 257). As we have seen, the financial investment institutions have made to facilitate the fundraising function has grown over the last nine years. However, fundraising expenditures as a percentage of the total resource development budget has decreased 8.5 percent during the same period of time.

Table 3-2 shows a 1994 mean of 31.7 percent compared to 34.4 percent in 1985. This data would suggest that, although many institutions are currently spending more money on fundraising than ever before, it is at a decreasing percentage of the total development budget allocation.

Table 3-2
**Fundraising Expenditures: Percentage of Total Development Expenditures
by Enrollment Size**

Enrollment	1994 High	1994 Low	1994 Mean	1989 Mean	1985 Mean
Up to 500	42.2	19.0	34.6	26.4	33.0
501-750	39.7	11.4	28.4	32.0	37.0
751-1000	44.2	20.4	29.4	29.9	30.0
1001-1250	49.6	24.1	34.4	36.5	33.0
1251-1500	43.8	14.2	28.1	32.7	40.0
1501-2000	55.5	11.4	33.1	30.9	35.0
2001+	46.5	19.7	36.5	32.1	33.0
Survey Mean of All Groups			31.7	31.5	34.4

One key way to assess stewardship in the development office is to look at how much your institution spends to raise $1 of gift income. A useful study on this subject was completed in 1990 by CASE and the National Association of College and University Business Officers (NACUBO). The study confirmed the conventional wisdom that total fundraising costs usually run about 15 percent of the total amount raised. "This does not mean that a good fund raising program is by definition one that costs less to operate," the authors of this study state, and they caution that "fund raising efficiency should not be confused with fund raising effectiveness (1990, page 12)." The study recommends that institutions:

- measure results in terms of return on investment,
- differentiate between the costs of development, alumni relations, and other constituent relations, and
- measure dollars raised per staff member to help individual goal setting (1990, page 15).

When asked, "Please indicate the amount of money your institution spends to raise $1 of gift income," the average for Coalition institutions in 1994 was 17 cents. Table 3-3 shows a breakdown by enrollment size. If we look at the mean figures from the three fiscal years outlined in this data, Christian institutions have averaged 15 cents to raise $1 of gift income over the past nine years. This is quite acceptable when considering the results from the CASE/NACUBO study.

Table 3-3
Cost to Raise $1 of Income (Fundraising Expenditures Divided
by Total Capital + Operations + Endowment)

Enrollment	1994 High	1994 Low	1994 Mean	1989 Mean	1985 Mean
Up to 500	$ .29	$ .04	$ .14	$ .10	$ .15
501-750	.22	.01	.14	.14	.17
751-1000	.26	.01	.10	.10	.13
1001-1250	.27	.08	.16	.17	.31
1251-1500	.22	.05	.13	.13	.20
1501-2000	.51	.08	.23	.13	.06
2001+	.26	.08	.16	.09	.22
Survey Mean of All Groups			$.17	$.12	$.17

The Equipping of Staff

Building an effective development team is vital to success. From the development director to the office receptionist, all people within the fundraising division have access to and/or contact with the precious gifts God has given our institutions—our donors. Hiring an alumnus who had a bad college experience or filling a position with an abrasive personality can pull the development team apart and counter efforts to build positive relationships with the institution's constituents.

Significant consideration should be given when looking at a prospective development officer. Along with an understanding of biblical stewardship, it is important to look for individuals who share your institution's mission, are gifted communicators, and follow the example in Luke 22 of having a "Christ-like attitude to serve."

Jerald Panas, in his book **Born to Raise**, surveyed more than 2,700 professional fund raisers and listed what he found to be the top 10 attributes, skills, and characteristics to look for when hiring a fundraiser. They are:

- impeccable integrity
- ability to listen well
- ability to motivate
- high energy
- concern for people
- high expectations
- love for the work
- perseverance
- presence, and
- a quality of leadership (1988, page 131).

Professional Staff

Knowing the number of staff needed to fill the important roles within the development office can be a real challenge. For some institutions, the shop itself consists of no more than one professional with little or no secretarial support. These individuals typically handle annual and capital fund drives and are now becoming more educated in the field of planned giving.

On the other extreme, some development offices with generous budgets have a plethora of full-time professional staff who divide up the country and represent their institution in their assigned region. These types of offices usually bring with them a generous number of support staff to keep the overall effort organized.

Paul Wisdom tells us that "the best way to determine the effective number of staff...is first to look at the functional area you need to cover, then decide whether a single individual is required, or more, at a particular institution to cover each area, or whether one person can handle the several functions" (1989, page 154).

The most recent Coalition survey asked member institutions to identify the number of professional and clerical/secretarial staff found in the development office. As Table 3-4 indicates, the 1994 mean number of professional staff is 3.7 persons with a low of .5 and a high of 14.

Table 3-4
Professional Fundraising Staff (FTE)
by Enrollment Size

Enrollment	1994 High	1994 Low	1994 Mean	1989 Mean	1985 Mean
Up to 500	4.0	1.0	2.4	2.1	2.5
501-750	4.1	1.0	2.3	3.7	2.7
751-1000	6.5	.5	3.5	2.9	3.2
1001-1250	6.5	1.0	3.9	3.8	3.5
1251-1500	6.0	2.5	3.5	3.4	3.7
1501-2000	9.0	1.0	3.6	5.4	4.2
2001+	14.0	4.0	7.2	6.2	8.6
Survey Mean of All Groups			3.7	3.9	4.0

Peter Drucker, in his book **Managing the Nonprofit Organization**, claims that "most of us employ average individuals to perform at extraordinary levels of excellence," and that "identifying each individual's strengths and building on those by developing new skills and enhancing existing ones, is one of the best ways to create a powerful organization" (1990, page 147). These are good thoughts to keep in mind when building the development team!

Support Staff

Support staff play a vital role in coordinating and organizing the activities of the development office. In addition to their many responsibilities, support staff help to relieve the development officer of the day-to-day operations of the department in order to fully utilize his gifts in the field. While there are certain aspects of the job that require the personal involvement of the development officer, support staff can and should handle an abundance of tasks.

The quantity of support staff varied widely in Coalition schools in 1994, from a low of zero to a high of 8. Table 3-5 shows a 1994 mean of 2.4 persons compared to a 1985 mean of 2.6.

Table 3-5
Fundraising Clerical/Secretarial Staffing (FTE)
by Institutional Enrollment Size

Enrollment	1994 High	1994 Low	1994 Mean	1989 Mean	1985 Mean
Up to 500	2.5	.5	1.5	0.9	2.4
501-750	2.0	.7	1.3	1.8	1.9
751-1000	3.0	0	1.6	1.9	1.8
1001-1250	5.5	1.5	2.7	3.0	2.3
1251-1500	5.0	1.5	2.4	2.9	1.7
1501-2000	8.0	1.5	3.3	3.4	2.4
2001+	8.0	2.0	4.2	3.9	5.8
Survey Mean of All Groups			2.4	2.5	2.6

With fundraising goals continuing to climb, it is interesting to note the gradual decline in overall development staff over the last 10 years. Although not dramatic, this data does show a trend of departmental down-sizing.

Wesley Willmer conducted a study in this area 10 years ago and suggested (then) that "small colleges should employ from two to five resource development professionals with an additional two to five supporting staff." Willmer's research found that four persons, perhaps three in certain cases, constitute the minimum professional staff for an effective small college program (1984, page 614). Despite the more recent growth and sophistication of the field, Willmer's advice remains relevant today.

The Role of the Chief Development Officer

Luke 6:40 tells us that "a pupil is not above his teacher; but everyone, after he has been fully trained, will be like his teacher." This verse packs a powerful message to today's chief development officer (CDO). In addition to the many tasks that involve interaction with the board of trustees, the president, the vice president of development, and top prospects, the CDO has tremendous responsibility before God to create a working environment where development staff understand and practice principles of biblical stewardship.

But it's not enough for the CDO just to create such an environment. CDOs must instruct by example and demonstrate these principles in their day-to-day activities. If the CDO, for example, shows signs of being overwhelmed with a big goal and a tight deadline and decides to "pull out all the stops" and slip into the mode of crisis fundraising, it's time to evaluate his or her approach to development.

High CDO turnover hinders the ability to create an environment which fosters a biblical approach to fundraising. A recent survey of 54 top officers across the country showed that the average tenure of today's CDO is just 3.65 years (MacMillan, page 65). With high expectations and very large financial goals, it is very difficult for the new CDO to find the time to concentrate on re-tooling the development shop from a biblical perspective.

Finding the right person to fill this key position of leadership makes all the difference in the world. Romans 12 and II Corinthians 8 and 9 put the emphasis on honesty and integrity, and the book of Luke addresses having a "Christ-like attitude to serve." These and a host of other qualities should be evident in all staff, but modeled through the character of the CDO.

Despite high turn-over in the industry, the majority of men and women who fill the position of CDO do have a background in development. Table 3-6 shows that in 1989, 33.3 percent of CDOs at Coalition member institutions brought with them some level of fundraising experience (Willmer, page 65).

Table 3-6
Position Prior to Becoming Chief Development Officer

Prior Field	1989 Percent
Development	33.3
Business	20.0
Administration	13.3
Higher Education Administration	13.3
Faculty	8.8
Alumni Officer	6.6
Elementary/Secondary Education	4.4

Prioritizing the many "in-house" development tasks can be hard for the CDO, but it is imperative that his or her schedule be structured in such a way where significant time can be spent cultivating relationships with the institution's top prospects. A CDO's well-organized schedule can serve as an example and motivation for the entire development team by setting the pace for "out-of-office" donor cultivation and solicitation.

The challenge to put aside the day-to-day operations of the development office and focus on landing the big gifts is a struggle felt by many CDOs at Coalition institutions. In 1989, Wesley Willmer conducted a study that asked CDOs to rate the amount of time they spent in major donor cultivation. The results, displayed in Table 3-7, show that 96 percent of CDOs spend less than 50 percent of their time working with major donors, and 84 percent spend at least 60 percent of their time on other development office tasks (1990, page 67).

Table 3-7
Time CDOs Spend on Major Prospects

Percent of Time Allocated to Cultivation and Solicitation of Major Donors	Percent of CDOs 1989
10% or less	22
20% or less	39
30% or less	59
40% or less	84
50% or less	96

A good CDO brings a breadth of wisdom to his or her position. With increased sophistication in the field of fundraising, enormous campaigns, and the increased emphasis on utilizing planned gifts, today's CDO must be well-rounded.

Yet the typical CDO is far from considering himself or herself an "expert." Many CDOs know a fair amount about each function within the development department, but rightly leave the in-depth understanding to their trained staff.

The development office is becoming more and more reliant upon two functions within the field of fundraising: prospect research and planned giving. Unfortunately these are not areas where the typical CDO excels. Boyer and Love, in an article in **Fund Raising Management**, remind us that "prospect research has become the foundation for a successful development effort" (1990, page 64), and Paul Kling states that "today's top development officers can no longer afford not to understand planned giving" (1993, page 53).

Willmer's 1989 study verified the thoughts of Boyer, Love, and Kling. When asking Coalition CDOs where they felt they needed the most training to be effective in their role, the majority, 65 percent, conveyed a need for additional training in planned giving. The findings, as outlined in table 3-8, go on to show that 52 percent of CDOs need additional training in major prospect management (a task usually handled by the prospect research office), and 44 percent could use assistance in expanding their understanding of the function of prospect research (1990, page 68).

Table 3-8
Areas in which CDOs, Staff Need Additional Training (%)

	By CDO	By Development Staff
Planned Giving	65	48
Major Prospect Management	52	59
Prospect Research	44	81
Capital Campaign	43	41
Corporations/Foundations	39	52
Planning	31	39
Annual Fund	11	56
Other	15	13

For today's CDOs to be successful, it is imperative they follow and model God's teaching on biblical stewardship. With this as a foundation, we can consider four additional factors which Timothy Willard suggests contribute to the success of the CDO.

Educational Factors:

- successful completion of a bachelor's degree
- successful completion of a master's degree
- successful completion of a doctoral degree

Social Factors:

- participation in college extracurricular activities
- membership in service organizations
- pursuit of people-related hobbies
- participation in career-development activities

General Factors:

- broad work experience
- long advancement experience
- at least five years tenure at present institution
- at least three years in present job

Administrative Factors:

- yearly review of departmental goals
- yearly review of departmental objectives
- routine assignment of specific duties
- yearly review of job descriptions
- performance appraisal based on attaining objectives
- adequate opportunities for professional development (1985, page 38)

Cultivating the Heart of the Donor

Cultivating the heart of the donor may seem like an unlikely partnership of words, but it represents one of the greatest responsibilities we have as development professionals. Consider two points found in Matthew 6:19-21. First, the text states, "Do not store up for yourselves treasures on earth, where moth and rust destroy, and where thieves break in and steal. But store up for yourselves treasures in heaven ...." Some time ago I saw this biblical principle violated in a campaign proposal from a religious institution. The document told how a proposed new building would improve the image of the physical campus. There was no mention of what would take place within the confines of the building to further equip faculty and students to impact the world for Christ. With this important component missing, the donor would simply be investing treasure in an earthly monument. As we look at this verse from a development perspective, it is essential that we approach our donors with a clear presentation of the opportunity to extend God's kingdom.

The second portion of this passage gets to the crux of the point, "...for where your treasure is, there will your heart be also." When donors are moved to give to your institution to help further God's work, they not only part with a portion of their treasure, they entrust you with their heart. So often we forget to make this connection. Genesis 1:27 places greater priority on God's value of people. The importance of the gift, therefore, becomes secondary to the concern and interest for the individual.

How we steward the hearts of our donors once the gift has been made is of equal if not greater importance to the overall process of cultivation. An institution which practices good "heart stewardship" once a gift has been made is much more likely to see a growing number of donors who increase the size and frequency of their support.

Operations Gifts

Gifts to higher education tend to fall within three broad categories: operations, capital, and endowment. In 1989, the Coalition for Christian Colleges & Universities asked CDOs to evaluate the degree to which their financial goals might change in each of these three areas. The results were to be expected. As Table 3-9 shows, CDOs predicted that all fundraising goals would increase annually by more than 5 percent.

Table 3-9
CDOs' Assessment of Change in Dollar Goals (%) 1989

	Decrease	Maintain	Gradual Increase < 5% per year	Major Increase > 5% per year
Operations Gifts	3.7	9.3	33.3	53.7
Capital Gifts	3.7	11.1	13.0	72.2
Endowment Gifts	0.0	13.0	14.8	72.2

Gifts to operations serve as the life-blood for many institutions and have increased steadily for the past 30 years. The national average for all of higher education in 1993 showed an increase of 3.3 percent compared to a 4.3 percent increase over the year prior (**Expenditures in Fund Raising**, 1993, page 3). At Coalition institutions, similar growth patterns can be seen over the last nine years.

Table 3-10 shows how gifts to operations have increased and/or decreased at member institutions since 1985. You will see an interesting phenomenon—a minimal increase in giving at smaller institutions, a slight decrease at the larger schools, and an overwhelming increase in operations gifts at institutions with enrollments between 750 and 1,250 students.

Table 3-10
Operations Gifts Received by Enrollment Size

Enrollment	1994 High	1994 Low	1994 Mean	1989 Mean	1985 Mean
Up to 500	$1,219,814	$500,000	$916,346	$824,727	$751,954
501-750	1,300,000	501,929	978,460	990,999	849,232
751-1000	4,378,956	552,670	1,475,007	1,233,963	716,564
1001-1250	2,255,025	417,000	1,309,417	979,320	567,921
1251-1500	1,999,084	620,486	1,270,547	1,258,377	1,162,857
1501-2000	2,480,000	325,000	1,337,991	1,747,588	1,565,399
2001+	6,324,068	579,457	2,003,150	2,794,817	2,023,187
Survey Mean of All Groups			$1,333,899	$1,272,834	

It is likely that giving to operations will increase at a moderate rate for years to come. Experts with the Council for Aid to Education (CAE) don't see dramatic changes in unrestricted support on the horizon, but recommend that we keep our eye on Gross Domestic Product (GDP). In a publication titled "National Trends," CAE stated that "shifts in support for current operations tend to mirror shifts in Gross Domestic Product...and, without necessarily implying any causal relationship, GDP has been a good long-term predictor of gifts for current operations" (1993, page 3).

Capital Gifts

More than a decade ago, Joel Smith contributed a chapter, "Rethinking the Traditional Campaign," in Pray's **Handbook for Educational Fundraising**. Smith predicted what at that time seemed unimaginable—the billion-dollar campaign (1981, page). As we have seen, Smith's words have become reality at several of the oldest institutions in the country.

While Coalition institutions are not involved in capital drives of this magnitude, the vast majority of our institutions are involved in some phase of a capital drive. The Coalition collected data from member institutions on giving to capital projects in 1985, 1989, and again in 1994. The data, as outlined in Table 3-11, might surprise you. In an age where campus expansion seems so prevalent, the schools with less than 750 students and more than 1,250 students have experienced a decrease in capital support. Although institutions with enrollments of 750 to 1,250 are experiencing an overall increase in capital support, capital giving as a whole to Coalition institutions has decreased 21 percent since 1989.

Table 3-11
Capital Gifts Received by Enrollment Size

Enrollment	1994 High	1994 Low	1994 Mean	1989 Mean	1985 Mean
Up to 500	$1,000,000	$0	$335,139	$367,246	$123,907
501-750	638,488	49,673	188,726	291,465	321,501
751-1000	2,100,000	0	553,247	618,417	536,538
1001-1250	2,017,811	25,000	906,053	882,473	319,163
1251-1500	1,200,000	28,284	368,780	957,105	630,607
1501-2000	750,000	105,000	410,664	567,517	1,498,339
2001+	1,940,000	313,951	893,505	1,569,902	1,175,903
Survey Mean of All Groups			$527,133	$661,010	

Just a few words on campaign timing as it relates to stewarding the heart of the donor—it is not unlikely with the magnitude of today's campaigns and the condition of the economy, to see institutions spread their capital drives over three, five, even seven years. While this may be necessary in certain instances, it is not recommended. In addition to wearing out the volunteers, a lengthy campaign can exhaust the relationships you have worked so hard to build with your top prospects.

Remember the words of Proverbs 13:12, "Hope deferred makes the heart sick." If your capital drive has no end in sight, take action to assure careful "heart stewardship" of those who made significant financial commitments in the early stages of the campaign.

Endowment Gifts

Blair Dowden defines endowment as "those funds given to an institution that are invested and the income from which is used to support programs and scholarships" (1993, page 47). Dowden states that endowment "ensures fiscal health and stability" (1993, page 47), and Loessin, Duronio, and Barton, in a study from the University of Pittsburgh, connect a strong endowment with "effective management, evidence of past fund raising success, and a high level of voluntary support" (1987, page 21).

For Coalition member institutions, building a strong endowment has become the top priority for the development office. With an overall decrease in giving to para-church organizations, the uncertainty of the economy, and growing governmental concerns in providing federal scholarship assistance to students attending religious colleges and universities, many Coalition schools have long-term financial concerns. Building the endowment, therefore, is one way to hedge against future uncertainty.

The Resource Development Survey sent to Coalition member institutions in 1994 asked for data related to total giving toward endowment. The results were startling. Since 1989, gifts to endowment have increased 288 percent from a mean of $319,918 to a mean of $922,266 by 1994. While you may suppose that the larger gifts for endowment would be found at schools with higher enrollments, it is interesting to note that it was the smaller schools, those with enrollments of 501 to 1,000, who posted the largest figures in 1994.

Table 3-12
Endowment Gifts Received by Enrollment Size

Endowment	1994 High	1994 Low	1994 Mean	1989 Mean	1985 Mean
Up to 500	$200,000	$0	$72,696	$80,031	$116,074
501-750	14,000,000	0	1,855,873	177,816	182,056
751-1000	15,524,423	0	1,359,806	247,233	190,006
1001-1250	1,027,019	0	409,808	478,395	235,241
1251-1500	1,889,077	120,457	695,450	624,277	457,776
1501-2000	189,864	34,494	95,182	616,561	622,946
2001+	5,433,512	64,171	1,116,588	486,248	645,219
Survey Mean of All Groups			$922,266	$319,918	

The Donor's Response

Accounts of fundraising in the Bible most often occur within the framework of existing ministry relationships. Words like "partners" and "fellow workers" can be found throughout the New Testament. In the book of Philippians, for example, we read how Paul received support in Thessalonica "more than once" for his needs.

These same biblical concepts holds true at our institutions today. It is a rarity that we would receive a gift from someone with no ministry connection and even more unlikely that they would give repeatedly. Harold J. Seymore, in his 1966 classic work **Designs for Fund Raising**, places the establishment of strong relationships at the core of the development officer's objectives. In his first chapter, titled "What We Need to Know About People," Seymore says that "the business of fund raising is not about raising money, but about people," and that "knowledge of donor behavior and motivation is crucial to the practicing fundraiser" (1966, page 16).

In 1985, and again in 1989, the Coalition asked member institutions to identify the sources from which their operations, capital, and endowment gifts were received. As Table 3-13 communicates, the leading category was individuals.

In 1993, the Council of Independent Colleges (CIC), in conjunction with the Council for Advancement and Support of Education (CASE), published a joint study to analyze the pressures that small college advancement shops face in raising money, attracting students, and gaining friends (1993, page 1). In this study, CIC member institutions were also asked to identify their sources for support and, once again, the greatest emphasis was on individuals (1993, page 34).

Table 3-13
Gift Sources by Constituent Group (Excluding Tuition)

Constituency	1989 Percentage	1985 Percentage
Individuals	21.7	24
Churches	20.1	17
Alumni	16.1	14
Foundations	10.8	9
Trustees	8.9	11
Businesses	8.2	7
Deferred Gifts	7.9	7
Faculty/Staff	2.7	2
Parents	2.4	3
Other	0.6	3
Government Grants	0.5	2
Students	0.1	1
For-Profit Subsidiary	0.1	0

So how do Coalition institutions fare in regard to their sources of income within all of higher education? The 1993 national estimates show the estimated voluntary support of higher education to be 27 percent by alumni, 23 percent by non alumni individuals, 21 percent from corporations, 20 percent from foundations, 2 percent from religious organizations, and 7 percent from other sources (1993, page 2).

We know that individuals are the greatest source of income for our institutions, but what form of solicitation works best? Research conducted by Yankelovich, Skelly, and White, and commissioned by the Rockefeller Brothers Fund, confirms that the most effective fund raising technique is personal solicitation, "one person asking another for a contribution (1986, page 3)."

In a 1989 study of Coalition institutions, member schools were asked to rank their fundraising activities according to the amount of gift income generated. The findings, as shown in table 3-14, reinforce the emphasis on personal contact.

Table 3-14
Generators of Income (%) 1989

Source	Greatest income						Least income	
	1	2	3	4	5	6	7	8
Personal Contacts	76	12	5	3	1	—	—	—
Churches	12	25	9	15	11	1	—	—
Direct Mail	9	23	37	20	4	1	—	—
Area Representatives	3	7	3	3	9	—	—	—
Special Events	—	8	12	17	16	8	—	—
Telemarketing	1	24	28	16	4	3	—	—
Radio Advertising	—	—	—	—	—	—	3	1
Television Advertising	—	—	—	—	—	—	1	3
Other	1	—	—	4	1	1	—	—

Concluding Thoughts

The job of the development officer on Christian college and university campuses will become increasingly difficult in the years ahead. Opposing forces abound. In addition to the governmental concerns threatening the whole of Christian higher education, we are witnessing the death of possibly the most charitable generation of men and women who support Christian causes—our elderly. Those in line to fill their shoes, the baby-boomers, have yet to demonstrate that they will fill the void left by their parents.

Research shows that teaching on biblical stewardship is almost non-existent in our churches and on Christian college, university and seminary campuses (Wuthnow, 1994, page 141; Barna 1994, page 59; Price, 1992, page 27). The sad but true words of Robert Wuthnow echo loud and clear when he said, "It should come as no surprise that many Americans have little understanding of stewardship at all" (1994, page 141).

Although an uphill climb, today's Christian development officers have the high calling, as Little says, "to be about the work of Christ on earth in sharing what Scripture says, indeed commands, in living the life of stewardship" (1995). We represent a small, yet critical mass of professionals who have within our grasp the opportunity to model and educate our constituents in the principles of biblical stewardship every day.

Dian Little concluded her speech to Christian fundraisers with four direct challenges which I leave with you.

- Learn the Scriptural imperatives of this profession
- Stress the importance of including stewardship training in your schools curriculum
- Teach stewardship in your churches
- Disciple your donors on biblical stewardship and do not let secular methodology guide your ministry (1995).

RESOURCES

Barna, George. **Raising Money for Your Church.** Glendale: The Barna Research Group, 1994.

Boyer, J. and J. Love. "Adding Efficiency Without Adding Staff," **Fund Raising Management**, October 1990.

Dowden, G. Blair. "Development: Winning Strategies for Fund-raising Success." **Winning Strategies in Challenging Times for Advancing Small Colleges**. Ed., Wesley K. Willmer. Washington, DC: Council for Advancement and Support of Education, 1993.

Drucker, Peter, F. **Managing the Nonprofit Organization: Practices and Principles.** New York: Harper Collins, 1990.

Expenditures in Fund Raising, Alumni Relations, and Other Constituent (Public) Relations. Washington, D.C.: Council for Advancement and Support of Education, 1990.

Hubbard, David A. **Ten Commandments for Development Officers.** Washington, DC: Christian College Coalition, 1994.

Kling, Paul. "Planned Giving and Annual Fund Can Cooperate." **Fund Raising Management**, February 1993.

Lewis, Wilson, C. "Investing More Money in Fund Raising—Wisely." **Taking Fundraising Seriously.** Ed. by Dwight F. Burlingame and Lamont J. Hulse. San Francisco: Jossey-Bass Inc., 1991.

Little, Dian. Speech presented at the Christian College Coalition Senior Development Officers' Conference. Vancouver, British Columbia: February 25, 1995.

Loessin, Bruce, A., Margaret A. Duronio, and Georgina L. Barton. **Fund Raising Effectiveness in Higher Education**. Unpublished Study, University of Pittsburgh, 1987.

MacMillan, David, F. "Development—Building a Balanced Program." **Friends, Funds, and Freshmen**. Ed. by Wesley K. Willmer. Washington, DC: Christian College Coalition, 1990.

Pray, Francis, C., Ed. **Handbook for Educational Fund Raising.** San Francisco, CA: Jossey-Bass Inc., 1981.

Price, Cecelia Hart, Ed. **The Reluctant Steward.** Indiana: Christian Theological Seminary and Saint Meinrad Seminary, 1992.

Rodin, R. Scott. Speech presented at the D.I.A.P. Conference. Tampa, Florida: February 14, 1995.

Ronsvalle, John and Sylvia. **The State of Church Giving Through 1992.** Wheaton, IL: 1992.

Schmidt, J. David. "Developing Lifelong Relationships With Donors." **Money for Ministries.** Ed. by Wesley K. Willmer. U.S.A.: Victor Books, 1989.

Seymore, Harold, J. **Designs for Fund Raising**. U.S.A.: McGraw Hill, 1966.

Seymore, Harold, J. **Miscellaneous Memoranda**. New York: American Association of Fund Raising Counsel, 1960.

Vallet, Ronald E. **Stepping Stones of the Steward.** Grand Rapids, MI: Eerdmans Publishing Co., 1989.

Voluntary Support of Education, 1993: National Trends. Washington, D.C.: Council for Aid to Education, 1993.

White, Arthur, H. **The Charitable Behavior of Americans—Management Summary.** Washington, DC: Independent Sector, 1986.

Willard, Timothy. "What Makes A Successful Chief Development Officer." **Currents**, July/August 1985.

Willmer, Wesley, K., Ed. **Friends, Funds, and Freshmen.** Washington, DC: Christian College Coalition, 1990.

Willmer, Wesley, K. "Stewardship: A Key Link to Commitment and Ministry," **Sundoulos.** California: Talbot School of Theology, 1995.

Willmer, Wesley, K. **The Small-College Resource Development Challenge.** Englewood Cliffs, NJ: Prentice-Hall, 1984.

Willmer, Wesley, K., Ed. **Winning Strategies in Challenging Times for Advancing Small Colleges.** Washington, DC: Council for Advancement and Support of Education, 1993.

Wisdom, Paul, E. "Another Look at Costs." **The President and Fund Raising.** Ed. by James L. Fisher and Gary H. Quehl. New York: Macmillan, 1989.

Wuthnow, Robert. **God and Mammon in America.** New York: Free Press, 1994.

About the Author

ADAM J. MORRIS has devoted his career to working in small college advancement and has received widespread recognition for his involvement in the non-profit sector. In 1989 Morris received of the Southern California Carnation Award for outstanding leadership in fundraising and volunteerism. Morris also received recognition from former President George Bush and was granted a national "Point of Light" award for his significant service to the community.

More recently, Morris co-authored the chapter "Glancing Back Briefly to Move Forward Confidently" with Dr. Wesley K. Willmer which appeared in **Winning Strategies in Challenging Times for Advancing Small Colleges***. Adam Morris is currently the director of capital projects and was previously director of annual giving at Biola University. He resides in La Habra, California, with his wife Faith and sons Caleb and Joshua.*

Chapter 4

The Alumni Connection

JEFFREY J. KRIMMEL

Many alumni offices today are facing an identity crisis. They are attempting to decide whether they are part of the development program, raising money and cultivating alumni, or purely a service activity which supplies support and programs aimed at simply helping alumni. Many alumni directors feel caught in a tug-of-war over planning programs to assist in fundraising and meeting the real needs of alumni regarding life after college. Is it possible to accomplish both goals in an honest and practical way?

Why do alumni offices exist? Where should they be headed in the future? What difference does the Christian college and university context make in their management? These are some of the questions this chapter will try to answer as it takes a careful look at the vital role the alumni office plays in the Christian college and university community. The chapter will discuss the goals of the office and the process of developing and maintaining good will and support from alumni. The alumni office has and will continue to have an increasingly important role in making genuinely supportive alumni out of sometimes dubious students. By reviewing the history of alumni programs, putting that history into a Christian context, and providing a framework and ideas to guide other programs, this chapter should function as a useful, encouraging document to colleagues in alumni work at other institutions. Let's first take a brief look at the history of alumni relations in general and the theory behind the office.

A Brief History of Alumni Programs

In the late 1700s and early 1800s, several schools began to realize a need to organize alumni as a united group in order to gain from these men and women the influence and patronage they could give back to their alma maters. In 1821 Williams College created a society of alumni to gain their support for improving the school, as well as the protection they could provide through their clout in the community. Through the creation of these alumni organizations, several spin-offs came into existence: a much more formal organization of alumni groups/clubs developed wherever a pocket of alums existed, and an organization, usually on campus, or associated with the school, came into being to organize the smaller groups of alumni. As schools recognized the full potential of this segment of people, formal solicitation of alumni for financial support began.

At one point, arguments raged between many of the big schools as to whether alumni associations should be a part of the college or university administration or governed by their own boards, independent of the institution. According to Robert Forman's **Handbook for Alumni Administration,**

> Despite the endless debates, a consensus did emerge from these meetings, and that was the following summary of the nature of Alumni work: to develop motivated and committed alumni, properly informed so that they might be called upon to respond to the various needs of the university, whether this be in the form of financial support, counsel, or simply interpreting the university to various constituencies. Cultivation of Alumni, as well as their continuing education, is the principal objective of an alumni program. The Alumni directors all agreed that alumni must be treated as full partners in the educational enterprise, along with other segments of the university community (Webb, 1989, page 9).

The alumni concept became more than an idea; it became a critical mass of people who had the potential of providing untold benefits to the institution.

As institutions grew older and the number of alumni increased, this influence and potential increased. Many changes have taken place during the past 150 years to develop and refine the purposes and programming behind alumni offices, both in Christian and secular institutions. Alumni offices have become more sophisticated in their ability to keep track of alums, provide necessary programming, and cultivate alums into active supporters of the college or university. Today, there is renewed interest in rededicating institutional support of the alumni programs, because of the distinct awareness that alumni are a priceless resource which can benefit the institution in numerous ways. Tables 4-1 and 4-2 show how that support is being realized in the areas of "Alumni Office Professionals" and "Alumni Office Expenditures" in institutions across the country.

Table 4-1
Alumni Office Professionals (FTE) by Enrollment Size

Enrollment	1989 High	1994 High	1989 Low	1994 Low	1989 Mean	1994 Mean
Up to 500	1.50	1.00	0.30	0.00	0.84	0.61
501-750	1.00	1.00	0.00	0.50	0.83	0.81
751-1000	1.30	2.50	0.30	0.50	0.88	1.02
1001-1250	2.00	1.00	1.00	0.50	1.17	0.90
1251-1500	2.00	2.00	1.00	0.25	1.40	0.89
1501-2000	3.00	2.00	1.00	0.50	1.38	1.21
2001+	2.00	3.00	1.00	1.00	1.30	1.44
Survey Mean of All Groups					1.10	0.97

Although a slight reduction in alumni professionals has occurred over the past five years, staffing continues to be strong. Dollars for alumni programs and activities continue to rise.

Table 4-2
Alumni Office Expenditures by Enrollment Size

Enrollment	1989 High	1994 High	1989 Low	1994 Low	1989 Mean	1994 Mean
Up to 500	$66,832	$80,000	$2,400	$0	$31,197	$35,085
501-750	99,724	150,000	5,646	0	44,622	60,485
751-1000	118,794	115,089	24,534	20,000	58,662	67,853
1001-1250	113,141	148,682	35,000	25,000	77,463	90,057
1251-1500	129,480	157,278	62,500	25,000	95,718	77,643
1501-2000	259,806	285,602	66,112	13,000	152,617	108,062
2001+	410,000	604,654	92,656	45,000	157,473	248,153
Survey Mean of All Groups					$75,599	$89,831

The Christian College and University Context

Knowing that the above benefits are available for the asking, how should the Christian college or university approach alums? Do Christians have the right to plan and execute programs and strategies aimed at cultivating persons to give during the next phonathon, receive the next direct mail letter, or entertain the president regarding a campaign pledge? It is tempting to slip into the mentality that says, "If we do this and provide that for alums, they will thus feel an obligation to support the college." And sometimes without even realizing it, alumni offices begin a process that seeks ways to manipulate people into giving rather than encouraging them to give freely from their hearts. For the Christian alumni director, alumni who give and participate freely should make all the difference in the world. "The challenge is to discover alumni motivation and determine how to translate their interest into volunteer roles that are meaningful to the alumni and valuable for the college" (Rodriguez, page 132).

In the book **Money for Ministries**, J. David Schmidt reviews several myths which western culture embraces, but which can cause pressures that strain godly relationships:

- Bigger is better. "Growing your mailing list even if you have a lot of low-involvement supporters."

- Quicker is better. "Go for the quick one-time gift. We're in fundraising, not here to educate our supporters."

- Absolute values cannot be known or agreed on. "Some passages of Scripture simply can't be applied to our situation."

- Waste is a part of life. "Donors are expendable. If they're offended by our practices, so be it. There's more where they came from."

- The bottom line is everything. "Ample income to meet needs and growth is of higher priority than how we get there" (1989, page 190).

All too often we allow these "norms" to taint our thinking and put us into a position of tampering with the priorities God would have for each individual donor. Soon we find ourselves placing more importance on the gift than the giver. "It is usually the major donors who get the special attention and private dinners with our organization's president, not the widows who give $5 faithfully each month out of their social security checks. When was the last time you saw an organization honor a widow who pledged $10 a month? We assign value to people based on the size and frequency of their gifts" (Schmidt, 1989, page 191). We are reminded of Christ's economy when we read Mark 12:41-44 (NIV):

> Jesus sat down opposite the place where the offerings were put and watched the crowd putting their money into the temple treasury. Many rich people threw in large amounts. But a poor widow came and put in two very small copper coins, worth only a fraction of a penny. Calling his disciples to him, Jesus said, "I tell you the truth, this poor widow has put more into the treasury than all the others. They all gave out of their wealth; but she, out of her poverty, put in everything—all she had to live on."

Have you ever experienced a campaign which has been won financially, but lost emotionally and spiritually? The "big dollars" were all accounted for but the victory's shallow emptiness seemed to fade the joy and excitement of the completion of the goal. Lists were made, programs executed, people seen, and the dollar goal accomplished, but something was missing. Something was lost in the process!

On the other hand, have you noticed successful campaigns, where the donors (whether alumni or others) were honestly excited about the mission of their college or university and challenged to stretch their faith by giving sacrificially; because of God's work in the lives of such folks, the financial goal was met. What a sweet victory and job well done!

You see, it comes down to a matter of perspectives. Do we launch off with only our own goals in mind, or are we willing to incorporate the plan God has for our colleges and universities and those who will support the project in one way or another? The number one goal of alumni relations should be to provide alumni with the opportunity to become involved with the institution's unique and special ministry and to offer them the chance to grow spiritually through sacrificial giving of their time, talents, and resources. Our Lord who owns the cattle on a thousand hills will work through us to provide the resources for whatever fundraising He deems necessary, but He is first interested in the spiritual welfare and growth of those who become involved. Therefore, our first goal is to provide opportunities and programs which will lead to a clear vision in our alumni of the exciting ministry occurring on our campuses. Secondly, we should provide information and opportunities for involvement on and off campus which will stretch their faith and provide the support all colleges and universities need. It's a natural - allow alums to see and become involved with the exciting things God is doing on campus and watch their full support come shining through.

The Process of Developing Committed Alumni

Developing active, supportive alumni does not happen overnight. Like any other significant experience in a person's life, initial decision and continuing commitment usually occur over a period of time and circumstances. Many people, events, and programs will touch a person's life before he or she comes to the point of decision. Producing alumni who will stand behind a college or university and be available to serve and give of themselves when called upon takes careful planning by the alumni office and the nurture and encouragement of many others on campus. Developing strong alumni support is a process which begins while a student is on campus and continues through the years after a student becomes an alumnus.

Building strong alumni takes the participation of more persons than just the alumni director. The process begins with the first person who introduces the prospective alum to the institution and develops through the years to come. From graduation day alumni relations attempts to bridge the miles between alumni and campus in order to continue a feeling of closeness, involvement, and belonging in the campus community. It would be unfair for faculty or administration to place all blame on the alumni office for alums who seem to care less about their alma mater after commencement day. Just as a large percentage of a child's personality and value system develops during the first few years of life, so the value and appreciation a student develops for his or her college or university during their relatively brief time on campus depend on all their institutional interactions. What occurs while they are students on campus will far outweigh any programming implemented once they are gone! Let's take a closer, step-by-step look at the Committed Alumni Decision Process.

The Committed Alumni Decision Process is an ongoing one which begins when an individual is first introduced to an institution and continues the rest of his or her life. The continuum illustrated here in Figure 4-1 points to the interrelationships between various peoples and departments on campus and off and the alumni office, with a potential student/alumnus response. The process points clearly to the fact that more than just the alumni office should be involved with developing committed alumni. The process requires the combined effort of many people throughout the years.

Figure 4-1
The Committed Alumni Decision Process

	Prospective Student/Alum Response	Alumni Office Role	College Role
Stage 1	no awareness	alumni recruitment volunteers	
	initial awareness		Public Relations
	awareness of general info/admissions	networking	Admissions
Stage 2		student alumni association	Fac./staff/admin.
	positive attitude developed identification with school graduation	*senior challenge *phonathon *homecoming *miscellaneous programs	
Stage 3	participates in alumni activities (homecoming, clubs, etc.) becomes active/ supportive alum	alumni newsletter	College/University provides financial/personnel support to alum office
	understands mission/ personal responsibility	homecoming	College magazine
	increases support in: *time *money *resources	alumni clubs	President's involvement and recognition
	joins alumni council/board supports school's mission sacrificially	alumni tours alumni ID card	Board of Trustees
		networking alumni council alumni fund *giving clubs *major clubs *planned gifts special projects sharing the vision	

Stage 1

The first step in the process is the introduction of the college or university to a prospective student who knows nothing about the institution. This usually occurs in one of several ways, including but not limited to the following: a friend, parent, college fair, etc. Obviously, it is important that the person making the introduction be someone the student respects. If an admissions representative is that first contact or is eventually used in the process, it is very important that a clear and honest picture of the institution be presented. Getting a future alum off on the right track means that his or her perception of your school needs to match the reality of the school as closely as possible. If a prospective student chooses your college or university because of its high ratings in a particular area of study or environment, then arrives on campus and discovers a gross over-rating, the experience will not serve to enhance development of a supportive alum. Many schools set themselves up for a fall, because they've raised the expectations of the student unrealistically or painted a picture of the college or university which is simply not accurate! A sensitive balance is necessary as admissions personnel attempt to "sell" the school, and care must be taken not to set students up for a disappointing let-down when they step onto campus. It is always much more positive to discover things are actually better than expected.

As Figure 4-1 illustrates, the college or university should make a well-balanced effort to use its professional offices to introduce itself to the community and to the targeted audience which will be most interested in what the college or university has to offer. Simultaneously, the alumni staff will want to work diligently to provide alumni who can speak from experience about their thoughts and feelings concerning the advantages of the institution. Hopefully alumni who are working in fields related to the prospective student's interests can be placed in contact with the prospective student. "Robert Forman suggests, 'Alumni are, without question, the single greatest resource a [college] president has. They not only provide needed funds, but recruit students, offer new and innovative ideas, and communicate to various constituencies'" (Rodriguez, page 131).

Here is where a well-coordinated "networking" system can make a big difference. Alumni relations, many times in conjunction with the career center, can accomplish several positive outcomes through the use of a good networking system, utilizing alumni around the world in an effort to make available contacts for job placement and student recruitment, among other things. Having willing alumni organized geographically and vocationally will allow the alumni office to plug a prospective student into one of the most convenient and helpful experiences he or she will have when choosing a school. At the same time the institution is reinforcing in the mind of the alum the value of his or her college or university experience. And so the many-faceted process of strengthening alumni association members has begun even as a new prospective student/alum gets off on the right foot.

Orchestrated properly, the college or university in Stage 1 will blend a mixture of its professional offices' services, including public relations, communications, and admissions, with the personal touch of alumni volunteers, whether they be parents or alumni with similar vocational interests. Together the college or university and volunteers should enhance the "student response" with a clear and accurate vision of what the institution will provide the student in the years to come.

Sometimes the vision is not so clear, perhaps due in part to an uncoordinated strategy for communicating the institution to its clientele. "Part of the difficulties documented here have their root in the fact that in many Christian organizations, there is no unified strategy for clientele communication. One person prepares audiovisuals, another writes the appeal letters, and still another edits the magazine. This problem is only compounded when these staff members are housed in different offices or departments. It is no wonder donors are ill-informed, in spite of the volume of communication they receive. There is no common message" (Engel, 1983, page 31). Thus it is imperative to work toward sending out a clear, common message.

Stage 2

The next stage in the decision-making process occurs while the student (future alumnus) completes his or her four or so years of college. The time spent on campus interacting with faculty, staff, and administration will impact, more than anything else, how the individual will feel about the school long after graduation day. If the student perceives a caring faculty and a trustworthy administration doing their best to provide an excellent education in a Christian context, chances are that student will turn out to be a caring and dedicated alumnus.

During Stage 2 the alumni office can offer many activities and programs which will encourage student support and identification with the college or university. Many of these programs will develop a deep sense of understanding regarding why the college or university needs alumni support and produce a high percentage of current alumni participation. Students involved in student alumni association programs like the phonathon or senior challenge develop not only an understanding of the significance of supporting the college or university, but more importantly, they in time persuade themselves that it is important to support the college or university when they become alums.

Let's take for example an annual phonathon program. Typically this event is run by the annual giving office. In most cases numerous volunteers are needed to call alumni, friends, or parents during a period of several weeks, thus creating a tremendous opportunity to involve student volunteers. Built-in incentives such as T-shirts, food, or free calls for each night the students work are well worth the expenditure! Not only does this provide the opportunity to orient students to the importance of giving financially to the college or university, but they in turn relay the message to hundreds of donors. Each time a call is made, the student volunteer puts into his or her own words why the college or university needs to be supported. Not only are donor dollars being raised, but, in a very personal way, the importance of this effort is being instilled in the thinking of student volunteers.

Another effort which works well, and in much the same way, is the senior challenge program. This event provides the entire Senior class with the opportunity to hear, from a fellow classmate, a face-to-face explanation of why alumni support is so important to the ongoing mission of the school. Agreeing to support the college or university and hearing the explanation from other seniors both instill a deep commitment and understanding regarding the importance of responding in a supportive way as alumni in the future. Once students see the full picture and begin to develop a genuine understanding of why the college or university needs their support, most are excited and more than willing to get involved. Of course our hope is that their involvement as students will spill over into their lives as alumni.

Enlisting students as volunteers for homecoming, parents' weekend, and class reunions also encourages student involvement. Hundreds of students may become involved in alumni activities this way, serving two purposes as alums and students come together. First, the alumni who return to campus for a special event have the opportunity to interact with current students. Many alumni are very concerned about the changes which naturally take place on campus after they leave. Their fear is that the college or university is not what it used to be and not accomplishing the mission (especially on the Christian college or university campus) that it once did. Hopefully, having the opportunity to meet present-day students will reinforce the fact that, although the way things are done may have changed somewhat, the product is still as strong as ever! Usually alums are greatly encouraged when given the chance to talk to a student about his or her experience. Thus, using student volunteers at homecoming or student callers during the annual phonathon gives thousands of alumni personal contact as well as encouragement regarding the mission of the school.

On the other hand, the alumni often reciprocate by showing students their example as supportive alumni, perhaps by making a worthy pledge at phonathon time or through their willingness to get involved with other programs. This interaction points out to students that these people really do value the time they spent at the institution and desire to do their part in providing others with the same valuable experience. Thus, an important exchange of perceptions and encouragement takes place. The alumni are encouraged by the students they meet, and the students are impressed with the genuinely interested and committed alumni with whom they talk.

Here are other program ideas which serve to strengthen alumni and student commitment to the school:

- **Senior Seminars on Survival (S.O.S.)**—This program brings back to campus alumni from various vocations such as banking, real estate, insurance, auto sales, and personnel or human resource vocations in an attempt to help seniors understand practical and personal areas of adjustment they will soon be facing.

- **Senior Breakfast/Awards**—This program provides the opportunity to have the president of the college or university, alumni director, and alumni association members give one last word about the new relationship between graduating students and the college or university. The alumni association might also recognize a graduating senior who already has displayed exceptional leadership and school loyalty during his or her years as a student.

- **Diplomats Program**—Students are a great resource when it comes to speaking to high schoolers about the college or university. Students are the college or university's product, so what better way to encourage prospective students, while nurturing current students to become genuine advocates of the institution and future dedicated alumni?

- **Student Testimonials**—Students who are willing to share their experiences with alums through council meetings, dinners, newsletters provide the much-needed evidence alumni desire while they are evaluating the degree of their own involvement.

Getting students involved and providing them with a positive experience and the best education possible are priorities while they are alumni in residence. As students grow in so many areas on campus, alumni offices will want to be sure one of those areas involves student commitment to and positive feelings about the institution. There will never be another opportunity like the one while they are at home!

Stage 3

Stage 3 of the process, if blended properly with the previous two stages, doesn't miss a beat as students become alumni and exit the institutional halls. At this time in the process it is crucial that names of seniors are listed properly in alumni files and that seniors feel welcomed to the alumni association. It is the job of the alumni office to extend a heartfelt welcome, as well as an open invitation to return to campus any time. The use of an alumni ID card can help establish the invitation to new alumni. In the weeks following graduation, a personalized letter welcoming them to the alumni association and offering a personalized alumni ID card are nice touches. The alumni ID card should invoke special alum privileges regarding such college or university facilities and programs as the library, swimming pool, fitness center, career development, and sporting events.

By offering the above, the college or university helps to establish a balance between asking and giving. Many alums will never use college or university resources, but knowing they have been offered by their alma mater helps cement an ongoing relationship with the school.

Many other avenues can be used to keep alumni informed and in touch with the college or university. One of the biggest events of the year occurs homecoming weekend. Features such as class reunions, alumni banquets, sporting events, and special theme-related activities make this an ideal time to invite alumni to return to campus. To assure a successful turnout, alums should be reminded three or four times to place the event on their busy calendars. Initial publicity and/or ads should begin three to five months before the scheduled date. Taking into consideration the special needs of your alums, such as providing easy access for older alums and childcare or children's activities for younger alums' children will be very much appreciated and make the day an even bigger success.

A regular schedule of off-campus alumni gatherings also should be incorporated into the alumni office calendar of events. Alumni chapters or clubs should be established wherever a pocket of alums lives and wherever a willingness exists on the part of one or two alums to spearhead the group's activity. Key local alumni are especially important for small alumni offices, since a single-person office cannot arrange for all the details of club meetings around the nation and world. It is vitally important that each chapter have its own leadership to encourage and motivate alums in that area to participate and help with the organization.

Alumni clubs or chapters are a terrific way to invite faculty or administration to bring a piece of campus to many locations miles away. A popular professor or the president of the college or university who hosts an off-campus event shows in a very real and practical way that the institution still sees alumni as an important part of the overall college or university community.

The alumni newsletter is another crucial way to keep alums informed and feeling as though they are "in the know" regarding campus events and environment. Alumni must see firsthand the product or results of the college or university's efforts. That means reporting back to alums the educational and spiritual growth which is currently taking place on campus. Colleges and universities cannot assume alums will believe that all is well with their ministries just because the institution says so. Newsletters should be filled with human interest stories capturing the essence of what Christian colleges and universities hope will occur on campus. Articles from students, faculty, and administrators which genuinely point to the fact that the Lord is accomplishing something special on campus have a much greater impact than reports from administration that all is well. In a day and age where most persons under age 40 have been taught to question authority, to compare organizations, and to analyze what they have learned before making a decision, vague illustrations and references to past record just will not do. The under-40 group will be unmoved by less than firsthand fact. Schools need to provide concrete facts as well as individual testimony to earn new alumni support through the years.

Dr. James F. Engel, distinguished professor of management resource and strategy and director of International Institute of Leadership Development at Eastern College, says,

> ...the younger generation in particular has different values and expectations. For example, the traditional 'romance of missions' is not likely to have the appeal it did for their parents and grandparents. Instead, there is greater concern about accountability and results in terms of changed lives. Some organizations, quite frankly, may not have a ministry which has a sufficient cutting edge to attract support from this emerging generation. Suffice it to say that increasingly, financial support must be earned, not merely requested or assumed (1983, page 17).

Thus, as programs or newsletters are prepared, it is increasingly important to give evidence that what the institution is doing is affecting lives. If alumni support is to be based on conviction, alums must be provided with the information, evidence, and opportunity they need to make a decision to jump on board!

At the same time, the college or university leadership must be committed to providing adequate financial and personnel support to the alumni office. This support is a must if the proper information and groundwork is to be laid. Without the finances and personnel available to plan programs and to distribute the necessary information to thousands of alumni, the information they must have to make further commitments will not be available. And as Dr. Engel said, "The under-40 segment are not likely to take claims at face value" (1983, page 13). In other words, it is becoming more and more apparent that in order to communicate our institution's needs, we need to do more than simply state them! As noted in the beginning of this chapter, a process occurs which incorporates both experience and concrete evidence and determines the degree of support alumni will offer. That process, shown in Figure 4-1, is one which begins as a person is first introduced to the college or university and lasts a lifetime. It involves and incorporates all aspects of the college or university community that touch a student's life while he or she lives on campus, as well as all programs, events, and literature which alumni receive after leaving the college or university community. Together, the information received and experiences shared develop the individual into the kind of supportive alumnus the college or university has earned. And although a community effort is required, it is the responsibility of alumni relations to be certain that committed and dedicated alumni are being developed and plugged into the mission of the school.

Alumni relations is not simply an office which supplies routine activities and gives occasional awards. In the Christian college and university context, alumni relations plays an integral part in the process of bringing people (alumni, as well as friends and parents) to a point in their lives where they feel led to sacrificially support the mission of the organization. The alum has had first-hand experience concerning the results college or university had on his or her life and has received evidence that the important mission of the school continues to be accomplished. As these puzzle pieces come together, a natural, spirit-led desire to support the college or university will transpire.

Other programs which help to involve and serve alumni include: tours, conferences, golf tourneys, networking programs for job searching, surveys, athletic events, merchandising, vanity license plates displaying college or university logo, insurance, credit cards, membership cards, cultural series, lectures/speakers (inspirational and educational), hospitality guides. "The involved person will likely imagine him or herself as a philanthropic leader, and therefore, give more. The uninvolved person will give less" (Rodriguez, page 131).

Of the above programs, one has been an especially helpful service to alumni in recent years. Although the alumni "networking" program has been touched on earlier in the chapter, it warrants reemphasis here. In cooperation with the career center, alumni offices around the country are tapping into the tremendous resource of the alumni body. Alums who are working in various fields in thousands of locations around the world usually are receptive to trying to help a fellow alum or graduating senior find a job. By coordinating alumni geographically and listing them categorically according to vocation, the alumni office and career center can provide an invaluable resource to their constituency. Networking capitalizes on the theory "it's who you know that counts."

As new and traditionally younger alums leave campus and begin to experience the ongoing programs, services, and information the alumni office provides, the process of commitment (see stage 3) should continue. A movement from simple participation in activities to involvement and understanding emerges. From there, alumni are challenged to consider what the Lord would have them do in the way of support for the college or university's mission. This may include spending valuable time on councils or committees, providing access to valuable resources for the college or university (available only through a particular alum), or making a financial commitment in a small or even significant way. In any event, the alumni office will have helped to bring an individual to full maturity of commitment to what God is doing through the institution. Remember, this commitment may be demonstrated in a variety of ways, not necessarily financial. But keep in mind the first goal—to encourage and allow alumni an opportunity to experience spiritual growth in their lives. The benefits institutions receive are simply an outgrowth of the new commitment level and should be a natural carry-through, or fruit, based on the alum's new commitment. If the annual giving and planned giving offices are tuned into this process, it should make their jobs easier and much more exciting and satisfying!

The ultimate goal is to have trustees leading the college or university towards its mission, the alumni office sharing the vision with students and alumni, and alumni giving sacrificial support to assure the continuance of the school's mission to students.

Obviously, the alumni relations role in this process is just one part of the whole picture. All employees of the Christian college or university, from custodian to academic dean, have an important part to provide for the alumni decision process to come to complete maturity. Alumni relations cannot be an office all to its own, uninvolved with the various aspects of many other departments on campus. The nature of alumni relations demands the overlapping of programs in a combined effort to bring students to maturity, and to encourage alumni to stretch themselves as God leads. If carried out in a well-balanced and spirit-led way, alumni relations will help to provide the vital support Christian colleges and universities so desperately need, while at the same time encouraging personal growth in the spiritual lives of alumni. Personal growth and college or university support are worthy goals. It is up to alumni relations offices to coordinate programs and information which will stimulate the process and allow those goals to be met!

Managing the Process

Obviously, it takes money and people to bring about a successful alumni program. In concluding this chapter it is appropriate to share with you some of the "nuts and bolts" of how other alumni relations offices are developing strong and capable programs. The Resource Development Survey collected alumni office data in 1989 and 1994 dealing with expenditures, personnel, mailing lists, and programming. The amount of money spent on alumni functions is listed in Table 5-3 as a percentage of total resource development expenditures (development, public relations, alumni, and admissions).

Table 4-3
Alumni Office Expenditures:
Percent of Total Resource Development Expenditures by Enrollment

Enrollment	1989 High	1994 High	1989 Low	1994 Low	1989 Mean	1994 Mean
Up to 500	15.9	10.4	0.9	0.0	7.3	7.0
501-7501	15.3	20.1	1.1	1.1	7.8	8.0
751-1000	24.5	20.4	4.5	2.5	10.1	9.2
1001-1250	12.5	12.1	5.2	0.0	9.1	8.0
1251-1500	14.2	22.1	9.6	3.1	11.6	8.8
1501-2000	15.7	16.7	5.5	1.3	11.9	8.3
2001+	17.6	21.0	7.0	5.3	11.0	11.8
Survey Mean of All Groups					9.3	9.6

Table 4-4 shows the size of alumni office clerical/secretarial staffs based on responses to the CCCU Resource Development Survey.

Table 4-4
Alumni Office Clerical/Secretarial Staffing (FTE) by Enrollment

Enrollment	1989 High	1994 High	1989 Low	1994 Low	1989 Mean	1994 Mean
Up to 500	2.00	1.00	0.00	0.00	0.45	0.31
501-750	5.00	2.00	0.00	0.00	0.85	0.46
751-1000	1.50	2.00	0.00	0.00	0.73	0.63
1001-1250	1.50	1.00	0.00	0.00	0.83	0.80
1251-1500	1.00	1.00	1.00	0.00	1.00	0.64
1501-2000	3.00	2.00	0.50	0.00	1.31	0.93
2001+	2.00	3.00	0.00	0.00	1.20	1.30
Survey Mean of All Groups					0.85	0.71

Obviously the cost-cutting trend of colleges and universities has not spared the alumni office. While in some cases expenditures grew over the past years, many offices are experiencing cuts in personnel.

Table 1-10 on page 8 in Chapter 1 reveals the sizes of alumni mailing lists as reported by respondents. The wide range of mailing list sizes is governed by such variables as institutional size and age.

Responses to questions regarding alumni programs indicate participants were split on whether or not fundraising is a responsibility of the alumni association. Fifty-five percent said raising money was a responsibility, while 45 percent said it was not. Of the 55 percent who said fundraising was an alumni responsibility, only one third reported satisfaction with how the alumni association fulfills the responsibility.

Forty percent of the responding institutions reported they have a special alumni program for recent graduates. Several Coalition schools said they host no off-campus alumni meetings, while one of the largest schools reported holding 68 meetings annually. The mean number of annual off-campus alumni meetings was 10.3.

The range of responses to a question regarding what percentage of total gift support came from alumni in FY 1988-89 fluctuated between a low of 1 percent and a high of 70 percent. The mean response was 18 percent. Respondents reported that an average of 21 percent of alumni made gifts to their institutions during FY 1988-89, but responses ranged all the way from 2 percent to 56 percent.

Ranges for expenditures, professional and clerical staff, mailing lists and giving participation vary widely for many reasons. I have yet to meet the alumni director who would refuse more help or money to improve his or her program. But, in keeping with the goals Christ would have for each one of us as we work with alumni, we need to focus on individuals and their needs, rather than exclusively on institutional goals and agendas. I hope we all will rededicate ourselves to helping our alumni reach the goals God has for them; this will in turn benefit our institutions in ways we never dreamed possible.

RESOURCES

Engel, James F. **Averting the Financial Crisis in Christian Organizations**. Wheaton, IL: MDA, 1983.

Schmidt, J. David. "Developing Lifelong Relationships with Donors." **Money for Ministries**. Ed. by Wesley K. Willmer. Wheaton, IL: Victor Books, 1989.

Webb, Charles H. **Handbook for Alumni Administration**. New York: Macmillan Publishing Co., 1989.

Rodriguez, Charles G. "Alumni: Fanning the Commitment Fire." **Winning Strategies**. Washington, DC: Council for Advancement and Support of Education, 1993.

Reading List

Robert G. Forman, "The Role of Alumni Relations," in Fisher and Quehl, **The President and Fund Raising**.

Jon Van Tils, "In Search of Voluntarism," **Volunteer Administration**, Summer 1979.

Richard Michael Markoff, "An Analysis of the Relationship of Alumni Giving and Levels of Participation in Voluntary Organizations," Ph.D. Dissertation, University of Toledo, 1978.

Flora A. Caruthers, "A Study of Certain Characteristics of Alumni Who Provide Financial Support and Alumni Who Provide No Financial Support for Their Alma Mater," Ed.D. Dissertation, Oklahoma State University, 1973.

James F. Engel, **Averting the Financial Crisis in Christian Organizations**, 1983.

J. David Schmidt, "Developing Lifelong Relationships With Donors." **Money for Ministries**. Ed. by Wesley K. Willmer, 1989.

Charles H. Webb, **Handbook for Alumni Administration**, 1989.

Charles G. Rodriguez, "Alumni: Fanning the Commitment Fire," in **Winning Strategies**, Washington, DC: Council for Advancement and Support of Education, 1993.

About the Author

JEFFREY J. KRIMMEL has been active in university development and alumni relations work for more than 12 years, having held positions in planned giving, the annual fund, and alumni relations. Recently accepted as a career missionary with SEND International, Krimmel has been assigned to Alaska Bible College, where he will concentrate his efforts on equipping young people for ministry. He earned his undergraduate degree from Messiah College in behavioral science/Bible and his M.A. in interpersonal communications from Wheaton College. Jeff and Terry, his wife of 16 years, have three boys, Michael, David, and James.

Chapter 5

Eight Critical Topics in Enrollment Management

PETER HARKEMA AND DALE KUIPER

The **Wall Street Journal** issue of April 5, 1995, front-page story "Colleges Inflate SATs and Graduation Rates in Popular Guidebooks" is a telling look at the state of affairs in college enrollment management today. The article details the degree to which prominent institutions engage in number fudging and cheating to ensure inclusion in various guide books, particularly **U.S. News and World Report**. Most of us can identify with the pressures that lead admissions officers to manipulate the facts to achieve enrollment goals. We all have engaged in our own creative marketing and are probably grateful that our institutions aren't featured in the **Journal** or in local newspapers. What drives reputable institutions to engage in blatantly deceptive and unethical behaviors? The answer is simple: pressure to meet enrollment goals.

Whether the enrollment goal is prestige through more scholarship students or larger enrollments to increase revenue, enrollment managers are feeling the heat. Today enrollment management stands along side of fundraising as the most important strategic management need in higher education. This chapter is an attempt to help enrollment managers understand their role from a distinctively Christian perspective. What are some of the critical topics in the profession? How are we facing these issues as an institution? Is our institutional mission compromised by enrollment management activities?

As we listen to our colleagues, the nuts and bolts dimension of enrollment management is less on their mind than these broader questions of professional ethics, staff management, technology, or population changes. Thus, we chose to address eight critical topics in this chapter. They are:

- Developing a service perspective
- Cultivating an institution-wide commitment to participant cooperation
- Agreeing upon enrollment goals that match your institution's mission
- Interpreting demographic variables within the context of your institution's enrollment goals
- Equipping and challenging your institution with an enrollment research program

- Managing pricing issues effectively
- Responding to new and emerging technologies
- Committing to integrity and ethical behavior

These topics are complex and our response is incomplete. However, we hope that the issues discussed here sufficiently inform enrollment managers to look more carefully at how these topics impact the campuses of our Christian colleges and universities. Perhaps the chapter will lead to stimulating discussions within admissions staffs, trustee committees, or president's cabinets. We hope so. The issues involved are too critical to an institution's future to be ignored.

1. Develop a Service Perspective

For some of us, the premises of Total Quality Management (TQM) serve as a basis for developing an enrollment management system. For others, Christ's command to love one another provides a basis. Many haven't thought about why they do their work, other than to realize that the institution that employs them expects enrollment goals to be met.

In the early years of enrollment management practices, perhaps from 1975 until 1985, the focus was on marketing. What can we do to attract students to our campus? The perspective was one of self-interest and resembled for-profit marketing. As the academy came to realize the broader implications of enrollment management, thanks to people like Don Hossler (1984, 1986), Frank Kemerer, Victor Baldridge, and Kenneth Green (1982) and others, the notion that institutions who served their students with appropriate advising, good teaching, and necessary student services were those that flourished. Some institutions missed the point entirely and watched while their expensive recruits enrolled and then transferred to institutions that cared about their needs. Thus, as a service perspective entered the for-profit world through the brow-beating rhetoric of people like Tom Peters, it also came to be a common topic in enrollment management circles.

Isn't it great that, as colleges and universities with a common Christ-centered purpose, our work in enrollment management can claim as its core value a principle that is scriptural and not cultural? One wonders why Christian colleges didn't take the lead in introducing higher education to serving one another. Once again, the secular world stole our thunder. Too bad! However, now it's time to get busy developing our enrollment management staffs and campuses around this service perspective.

The Marks of a Beautiful Organization

A few years ago at a Coalition for Christian Colleges & Universities Enrollment Management Seminar, Dr. Peter Vande Guchte, at the time vice president for college advancement at Calvin College, presented his thoughts on the "Marks of a Beautiful Organization." Pete gleaned his wisdom from Robert Greenleaf's **Servant Leadership** (1977), Max DePree's **Leadership Is an Art** (1989), the New Testament, and his own experience. These marks are a helpful foundation for institutional enrollment management and staff management:

1. *Distinguish between contracts and covenants.* In a covenant, he says, we operate on the basis of understanding, agreement, commitment, and trust. Thus, although organizations need contracts to work well together, we must be in a relationship that is characterized by covenants. In a covenantal relationship, errors do not mean as much as in contracted relationships. One assumes forgiveness and a spirit of love in covenantal relationships.

   Think of how this perspective might change the attitude toward students on your campus. How about working with your staff? When an organization deals with change, conflict and developing potential in the spirit of the covenant, we achieve a radical departure from the strained, individualist perspective which typifies our society.

2. *Distinguish between organizational hierarchy and equity.* Organizational charts do not make a beautiful organization. A person's value is not based on rank. Beautiful organizations recognize the equality of personhood of individuals. Whether in the classroom, orchestra, or on the admissions staff, we accept each other's personhood, but not necessarily their performance. What a great basis for accountability and growth!

3. *Distinguish between performance and performance with joy.* Whether creating a work of art, fishing, or building a new building, there may well be more value in the process than in the end product. As we shape beautiful organizations, we must distinguish between performance alone— potentially ugly—and performance with joy, which celebrates the worker, the work, and the product.

4. *Add rewards and celebrations to planning and goal-setting.* The bottom line perspective of so many organizations is not enough. We need to give thanks to one another in (perhaps but not necessarily!) small but frequent celebrations and rewards. Max DePree in his book **Leadership is an Art** (1989, page 9), says, "The first responsibility of a leader is to define the task, the last is to say thank you." What a beautiful summation of a working relationship!

Consider these two examples of organizations practicing these marks of a beautiful organization. The first organization is the local Salvation Army office in Grand Rapids. Pete's wife, Jill, joined their staff and after a short time on the job, received a card signed by the entire senior staff telling her that she "was the focus of special prayer today at divisional headquarters weekly devotions." The cover of the note proclaimed the wonderful benediction of Numbers 6:24-26. Needless to say, she felt encouraged and more committed to her work. A similar act of encouragement happened within the Wheaton College admissions staff. Dan Crabtree, director of admissions, shared in a National Association of Christian College Admissions Personnel (NACCAP) newsletter that their staff prays for "a specific NACCAP college at each weekly staff meeting." Dan reports this has been a good experience for his entire staff. A servant-heart leads to a beautiful organization!

Building a Team

Recently at a video conference presented by Peter Senge, he spoke of a "chaotic" perspective of the universe. From this perspective, he concludes that managers and leaders are less likely to be in control. Therefore, says Senge, leaders must "let go of wanting to control," and let the natural visionary instincts of people emerge.

Certainly we could debate the theological ramifications of Senge's "chaos perspective," given our belief that the universe is firmly under the control of a Creator God. However, most of us also identify with complexity, sometimes bordering on chaos, in our enrollment management world. What does the future hold for our institutions given shifts in federal and state funding patterns? Will increasing diversity prove to be a benefit or a liability to enrollment? Will students continue to believe the benefits of Christian higher education are worth the costs? These and many other questions illustrate the dynamic character of our work. Under these circumstances, we must tap the vision of our coworkers and create genuine dialogues that uncover these visions. The best way to organize to accomplish such synergism is around the team model.

Jon Katzenbach and Douglas Smith in an informative **Harvard Business Review** (1993, pages 111-120) article discuss the "discipline of teams." The essence of a team, they say, is common commitment. Among their observations regarding teams, Katzenbach and Smith note that "at its core, team accountability is about the sincere promises we make to ourselves and others, promises that underpin two critical aspects of effective teams: commitment and trust." Covenants! A mark of a beautiful organization.

Peter Drucker (1988, page 75) says management is about human beings. "Its task is to make people capable of joint performance, to make their strengths effective and weaknesses irrelevant." As enrollment managers, we have the opportunity to create environments that encourage creativity and joint performance. If we fail to assume this role of institutional catalyst, we will miss the opportunity to teach our institution the complex character of enrollment management and what systems are necessary to respond to enrollment challenges.

It is clear that each campus has a unique answer as to how to best unleash the creative energies toward enrollment management solutions, but that initial step is to accept an institution-wide perspective.

2. Cultivate an institution-wide commitment to participation and co-operation.

A few months ago at a conference of admissions officers, a discussion developed about how to develop an environment of understanding with other campus people regarding the comprehensive nature of meeting enrollment goals. The admissions officers were sharing stories, particularly about student development staff, and the lack of sensitivity to admissions office needs and expectations in hosting prospective students for on-campus visits. The tone of the conversation, and the fact that many admissions directors spoke of similar frustrations, underscores that many campuses have a long way to go toward developing a comprehensive approach to enrollment management. Too many of us are stuck in turf battles about staff or budget allocations and are not serving our institutions well in advocating for solid institutional enrollment planning.

A Systems Perspective

Little information is available regarding how many institutions utilize a comprehensive enrollment management system. Noel Levitz reports that in 1992, only 10 percent of 602 institutions reporting said their chief enrollment officer held the title of vice president. Fewer than half (42 percent) of chief enrollment officers report to the president. Even more telling is that fewer than half (47 percent) of chief enrollment officers also supervised financial aid and 35 percent held responsibility for retention. Fifty-seven percent did report working with an enrollment management committee, but only half of these had responsibility for retention. Higher education is very slowly accepting a more comprehensive approach to enrollment management.

In their important study of leadership in higher education, Cohen and March (1974, pages 195-229) concluded that higher education can best be characterized as "organized anarchy." According to Baldridge and Deal (1983) power in higher education is diffuse and fragmented into departments and divisions. Often it can be a "collection of fiefdoms" (Graff, 1986, pages 89-101). In discussing communication systems within higher education that contribute to a "constrained environment," Gratz and Salem (1988, page 1) pointed out that most information is communicated "through telephone calls, chance meetings, memorandum, after committee meeting caucuses resulting in distortion and lack of information by key participants." What do these perspectives tell us about developing an enrollment management system?

One thing seems clear. Developing a system will be hard work and must be taken seriously by those endeavoring to accomplish such a goal. Unless the institution in its strategic planning identifies this comprehensive enrollment management perspective as necessary, and unless the president and cabinet affirm the need, positive results are unlikely. There must be an institutional commitment, not to a particular system or approach—many are possible—but to the need for broad institutional participation and cooperation.

Michael Dolence (1993, pages 23-24) in his pamphlet on "Strategic Enrollment Management" suggests there are eight "critical success factors." They offer a simple guide to institutions interested in building an institutional enrollment management system.

1. *Leadership*: Communicate a sense of importance and urgency. A successful system requires high levels of cooperation, coordination, and teamwork.

2. *Strategic Planning*: Institutions must be disciplined in producing decisions and actions that shape their nature and direction.

3. *Comprehensive*: Enrollment management systems are holistic processes involving virtually the whole institution.

4. *Key Performance Indicators*: These indicators must measure recruitment, retention, and operational performance.

5. *Research*: Rely on a steady flow of information on demographics, societal trends, price sensitivity, etc.

6. *Academic Foundation*: The academic program and policies of the institution form the heart of an enrollment management system.

7. *Information Technology*: A state-of-the-art information system is necessary.

8. *Evaluation*: Use evaluation in developing the system as well as monitoring its progress.

Comparative Data on Enrollment Management Organization and Cost

Enrollment management is an expensive piece of institutional budgeting. Most would agree that to not do sound enrollment management is even more expensive. One benchmark statistic that the Coalition for Christian Colleges and Universities (CCCU) and national organizations keep as a means of understanding the relative cost of enrollment management is the cost of enrolling a new student. In fall 1994, 41 CCCU institutions submitted data to help monitor the increasing cost of enrollment management. That study reports an average cost to recruit a new students of $1,502 compared to $1,417 in 1993. Williams Crocket 1993 National Enrollment Survey commissioned by Noel Levitz Centers Inc. reported the average for four-year private colleges was $1,505. The CCCU tracks admissions/recruitment data by enrollment size and also maintains benchmark data on the comparative size of admissions professional and clerical staff. Total admissions expenditures and staff size from the 1988-89 and 1993-94 CCCU studies are compared in Tables 5-1 through 5-4.

It is noteworthy that the mean "admissions expenditures" (see Table 5-1) increased over the five-year period more than $100,000 or 30 percent. In a more recent survey conducted with 47 CCCU institutions, it was reported that most of the increase in admissions expenditure is in advertising and postage expense. Table 5-2 reports only a slight increase in "admissions recruitment expenditure" as a percent of resource development. This should come as no surprise, because all of our institutions are adding resources to advancement/development functions.

Table 5-1
Admissions Expenditures (Including Salaries and Benefits, Travel, Media/Promotion, etc.) by Enrollment Size

Enrollment	1989 High	1994 High	1989 Low	1994 Low	1989 Mean	1994 Mean
Up to 500	460,196	393,661	77,600	127,000	227,499	243,280
501-750	472,000	520,801	92,000	211,000	267,274	339,058
751-1000	437,541	902,913	120,292	219,243	280,907	381,226
1001-1250	480,305	546,814	204,930	172,938	348,826	398,600
1251-1500	536,212	739,265	147,774	245,335	371,410	476,306
1501-2000	1,040,285	1,013,544	95,150	336,019	530,884	560,092
2001+	765,000	222,554	150,000	1,254,200	474,293	791,029
Survey Mean of All Groups					330,608	430,964

Table 5-2
Admissions Recruitment Expenditures: Percentage of Total Resource Development Expenditures by Enrollment Size

Enrollment	1989 High	1994 High	1989 Low	1994 Low	1989 Mean	1994 Mean
Up to 500	61.0	62.3	38.0	36.2	49.7	51.0
501-750	65.8	58.0	26.4	31.6	47.9	46.2
751-1000	62.4	56.0	20.6	36.9	45.8	46.7
1001-1250	60.0	61.1	25.8	28.3	41.4	41.7
1251-1500	61.1	67.6	28.7	43.6	43.8	49.4
1501-2000	50.5	76.1	19.4	32.0	36.7	48.6
2001+	43.9	71.6	26.8	27.3	36.2	39.1
Survey Mean of All Groups					44.4	46.4

Finally, Tables 5-3 and 5-4 show a shift up in recruiting/admissions professional staff of almost one FTE over the five years, but a much smaller .15 FTE increase in clerical/secretarial staff. Institutions are investing in the sales team and expanding their strategies to communicate personally with prospective students.

Table 5-3
Recruiting/Admissions Professionals (FTE) by Enrollment Size

Enrollment	1994 High	1989 High	1994 Low	1989 Low	1994 Mean	1989 Mean
Up to 500	7.00	9.50	2.00	2.50	3.81	4.30
501-750	7.00	6.50	2.00	0.00	5.54	4.20
751-1000	11.00	6.00	3.50	0.00	5.77	3.70
1001-1250	10.00	8.50	0.00	4.00	5.45	5.50
1251-1500	8.00	7.00	0.00	0.00	4.43	4.20
1501-2000	19.00	10.00	0.00	3.00	6.25	6.60
2001+	17.00	12.00	0.00	3.00	8.22	6.50
Survey Mean of All Groups					5.68	4.80

Table 5-4
Recruiting/Admissions Clerical/Secretarial Staff (FTE) by Enrollment Size

Enrollment	1994 High	1989 High	1994 Low	1989 Low	1994 Mean	1989 Mean
Up to 500	2.00	4.50	1.00	0.00	1.44	1.50
501-750	4.00	3.50	1.00	0.00	2.23	1.70
751-1000	5.00	4.50	1.00	0.00	2.47	2.00
1001-1250	4.00	4.50	0.00	2.00	1.90	2.60
1251-1500	5.00	6.00	0.00	0.00	2.71	2.60
1501-2000	6.00	4.00	0.00	1.00	2.36	3.00
2001+	8.00	7.00	0.00	0.00	4.15	4.00
Survey Mean of All Groups					2.46	2.30

It is clear that successful institutions will employ a comprehensive approach to enrollment management; and that developing the system will be hard work. Enrollment managers should also expect that the basic building block of the system—establishing institutional enrollment goals—is the critical starting point.

3. Agree upon enrollment goals that match your institution's mission.
How does the following driving analogy relate to your institution's enrollment goals?

> ***Police Officer***: *Do you realize that you are driving the wrong way on this one-way street?*
>
> ***Driver***: *Have you considered that the one-way sign may be pointing in the wrong direction?*

Which way is your college's one-way "enrollment goals" sign pointing? Does everyone on your campus—from the president and the board to your admissions counselors—view your enrollment goals as pointing in the same direction? In the *right* direction? Does that direction match what is called for in your institution's mission? Questions like these remind each of us of the need to develop our institution's enrollment goals with the resulting intent of traveling together on a journey that reaches goals that are consistent with the overall purpose of the institution.

Strategic Planning and Enrollment Goals

Effective strategic planning is fundamental to setting an institution's enrollment goals. Back in 1983, George Keller (1983, pages 143-152) suggested six features that distinguish strategic management for higher education. Strategic planning, according to Keller, 1) is active rather than passive, 2) looks outward—is focused on keeping step with the changing environment, 3) is competitive in nature, 4) concentrates on decisions, 5) is participatory and highly tolerant of controversy, and 6) concentrates on the fate of the institution above everything else. Since then, when revisiting this discussion, Keller (1993, pages 10-12) suggests that strategic planning has not always been successful, but goes on to cite four "powerful stimulants" that continue to make strategic planning both necessary and possible: external conditions are changing rapidly, demands for accountability to outside agencies are enlarging, financial strength has deteriorated for numerous institutions, and information technology has grown at a phenomenal rate.

Further consideration of any of these more recent "stimulants" quickly points to factors closely linked to enrollment management issues. It is clear that effective enrollment goals rise out of carefully considered strategic planning. An enrollment goal that is not guided by a strong, well-developed strategic plan could easily end up going the wrong way on a one-way street. And a plan that does not carefully consider enrollment issues is not strategic at all.

Setting Enrollment Goals

An enrollment manager must work to help insure that enrollment goals are owned by a broader group than just the admissions staff. Those with specific responsibilities for enrollment must nurture the support and understanding of the broader community. As enrollment managers, we often have information on both the internal and external environments that will most directly influence our college's enrollment goals. In this age of information it is our responsibility to make such information available to the decision-makers on campus. Sharing ideas and information is essential to pursuing the institution's strategic initiatives effectively. Empowering your campus with information will also assure the front-line staff—"those whose job it is to worry about enrollment"—that the entire community is supportive and understanding of the goals that we are *all* working towards.

Future enrollment goals must be set by considering past enrollment trends in combination with the college's vision for the future. Budgets and enrollment goals must be in balance—ideally fiscal needs will not mandate enrollment goals. One related question that has been and continues to be on the horizon is: *How (or why) should enrollment goals for non-traditional markets be evaluated?* Many colleges—including several within the CCCU—have growing enrollments from older-than-average, continuing education, graduate education, and distance education markets. As enrollment managers we must be careful that such programs not be evaluated in a different context than the traditional undergraduate program that has been at the heart of our college's mission. These markets and their resulting programs can add a great deal to the enrollment picture on a campus. But we must be ready to answer the question—"At what cost?"

Other questions that should be considered when determining enrollment goals include: *How does the decision to add or eliminate academic programs coincide with the college's enrollment goals?* and *How does (or should) a liberal arts college set specific enrollment goals for specific departments and programs?* The strategic planning decisions that involve these and other even more focused enrollment goals should include key enrollment managers and consider related market information. Questions such as these point to areas where decisions are oftentimes made outside of the enrollment management arena—in spite of the fact that any strategic planning and overall goal-setting would place responsibility for the answers and outcome within that very arena. It is essential that those responsible for attaining our goals also are given the opportunity to own the goals.

Measuring Enrollment Goals

Once enrollment goals are carefully set through a comprehensive strategic planning process, those goals must be stated and reinforced in both short- and long-term plans. Michael Dolence (1993, page 12) offers a helpful list of benchmarks, or "key performance indicators"—KPIs—that should be set in order to measure position against the competition, the success of strategies and tactics, and the relative position to past performance. KPIs can be set for recruitment, retention, and operational areas.

The one-way sign that signals your institution's enrollment goals must also be visible to and agreed upon by the entire community. There should be continued effort to ensure that the whole campus is headed in the same direction and that there is a campus-wide ownership for all enrollment goals and the activities that affect them. Given that new student recruitment is only one piece of the enrollment picture—although a significant one—it becomes quite clear that our enrollment goals must reach beyond the recruitment of new students. Our goals can and should be met through effective, deliberate retention efforts as well. The one-way street that we work so hard to get our new students to enter certainly must not change direction once they are on it!

Since 1980, enrollment managers have developed a heightened awareness for the importance of understanding demographic patterns as they consider enrollment goals. A focused consideration of key demographic variables is yet another critical topic to consider.

4. Interpret important demographic variables within the context of your institution's enrollment goals.

If you've ever heard Harold Hodgkinson, a demographer who became familiar to many higher educators in the 1970s and 80s, you know he often delivers stark reality in a humorous way. For example, he reminds us that "the discipline of economics has no forecasting methodology that can match the basic tool of the demographer: every decade people get precisely ten years older." Is demography destiny for higher education?

It's not good theology, but an issues panel commissioned by the Association of Governing Boards of Universities and Colleges says the answer is "yes." In their report, **Trustees and Troubled Times in Higher Education** (1992, page 9), they say that "demography is destiny for institutions of higher education. The children born each year are the youngsters who will apply to our colleges and universities 18-20 years later. Numerically, demographers have not favored higher education for the last decade, but institutions have been able to dodge the bullet by reaching out to nontraditional and older students. That alternative has been played out."

Hodgkinson, in his February 1993 report for the National Institute of Independent Colleges and Universities, **Independent Higher Education in a Nation of Nations** (1993, page 10), bluntly prophesies that "the best independent institutions of higher education are highly selective, and will fill their classes with no particular difficulty, even in states that will decline in youth over the next seventeen years. But for the majority of our 1,600 independent colleges and universities, between now and the year 2010, the options will be: 1) increase student diversity, 2) get smaller, and 3) move downward in the quality pool of applicants."

Each institution must interpret these prognostications within the context of its own mission and external circumstances. However, none of us can be so cavalier as to ignore the changes around us and the implications to the future. Must our mission be expanded? Are we prepared for diversity? Are faculty prepared to teach adults? Whatever your institutional context, there are critical questions to confront. Below, we attempt to briefly outline important demographic variables for enrollment managers.

Critical Demographic Variables

A. *High school graduates:* In their 1993 report, **High School Graduates: Projections by State 1992-2009**, the Western Interstate Commission for Higher Education reports that high school graduates declined 20 percent from 1979 until 1992. However, their data indicates a "baby boom echo" from children born in the 1980s and 90s. Public high school graduates will increase 34 percent from 1992 until 2008. There will be 9 percent more public high school graduates in 2008 than in 1979.

   When regional shifts are taken into account, along with the "close to home" character of most students' college choice behavior, the implications are more obvious for CCCU institutions. During this period, all regions increase in high school graduates, but the rate of increase varies greatly by region. For example, the increase is the greatest in the west which will experience a 65 percent increase. The south will increase 29 percent, the northeast 25 percent, and the northcentral 15 percent.

B. *Diversity of U.S. youth population:* If we consider just the increase in high school graduates in the next 13 years, enrollment planners can feel a sense of relief. However, most realize that the increase is just part of the picture. Perhaps for higher education the most important demographic shift is the tremendous increase in diversity among high school graduates. Hodgkinson reports that by the year 2000, 36 percent (up from 30 percent in 1992) of the U.S. public school population will be from minority groups. The increase is not equally distributed, and this factor bears heavily on enrollment planning.

By 2010, one third of the nation's youth will live in California, Texas, Florida, and New York. All of these states will have "minority" youth populations of more than 50 percent. In addition, New Jersey, Maryland, and Illinois will have more than 40 percent of "minority" youth. In states where many CCCU institutions are located, such as Virginia, Michigan, Ohio, Pennsylvania, Indiana, Massachusetts, and Missouri, there is virtually no increase in Caucasian youth.

Further complicating the enrollment management scene are differing college participation rates by race/ethnicity. The **Thirteenth Annual Status Report on Minorities in Higher Education** (1994) reports that "despite rising college enrollments, students of color continue to lag behind whites in their rates of participation in higher education. Only 33 percent of African-Americans, and 36 percent of Hispanic high school graduates ages 18 to 24 attended college in 1993, compared with nearly 42 percent of whites."

C. *Gender of college enrollment*: Most independent colleges and universities have experienced the increase in female enrollment that is reported nationally. Tom Mortenson, in the July 1994 issue of his research letter, **Postsecondary Education Opportunity**, notes that from 1959 until 1993 college continuation rates (rate of enrollment from high school to college) of males has increased 5.5 percent, but the rate of increase for females was 26.8 percent. The rate of high school to college continuation by decade is illustrated below.

Figure 5-1
Female College Continuation Rates 1960 to 1993

1960	37.9%
1970	48.5%
1980	51.8%
1990	62.0%
1993	65.4%

D. *Age*: Depending on who you ask, experts believe that the growth period in higher education with older students is either just past or still lies in the future. The aggregate answer to the question isn't as important to individual institutions as how they understand their institution's stake in the older student population. This has much to do with how institution's perceive their mission, competition, and local demographics.

One way for enrollment planners to look at this phenomenon is to consider the changing percentage of 18-year-olds. Data from the U.S. census indicates that in 1970 34 percent of the U.S. population was under 18. By 1980 this dropped to 28 percent and to 26 percent by 1990. Census data also indicates that from 1990 to 2000 the 35 to 54 age group (boomers) will grow 28 percent while the 25- to 34-year-old group will decline 15 percent. Harold Hodgkinson (1993, page 16) concludes from these data that "people over thirty represent the most important market for education. But people over thirty use education to advance their careers, which people over fifty seldom do." He asks, "How can independent higher education help people near or past the end of their careers become more fulfilled...?"

E. *Internationals and immigrants*: Most campuses have experienced growth among recent immigrant and international students. While these students represent a small part of our enrollments, changes are taking place within these populations that enrollment planners should not ignore. Obvious to all is the shift of immigrants from a largely European to an Asian or South/Central American population.

The Institute of International Education reports in the 1993-94 issue of **Open Doors** that the number of international students attending U.S. institutions has leveled off at 449,749. Of these, 264,693 or 59 percent were from Asia. This is the seventh consecutive year that Asians represented more than half of international student enrollment. However, the rate of increase is essentially flat which is in large part due to slightly fewer students from China, the country with the largest number of international students— 44,381 in 1993-94.

Consideration of demographic patterns underscores that managing enrollments is a complex institutional task. Institutions that do it well have accepted the fundamental need for data driven decision-making. Not only must institutions know the larger demographic shifts, but they must also know the shifts occurring in their markets that affect recruitment strategy, pricing, and retention.

5. Equip and challenge your institution with an enrollment research program.

Two trends have created powerful twin pressures in enrollment management. On the one hand we are pressed to keep enrollments steady or growing despite the ever-changing pool of potential applicants. On the other hand, we must also do so with limited resources. A data based enrollment management program with particular attention paid to research and information systems is an important step toward helping a college have an effective and efficient program.

A Data-Based Enrollment Information System

Institutional research can provide significant qualitative and quantitative information on all phases of the college's program. Critical to such a focus, though, is a good marketing information system. Easy access to information and data integrity are two critical foundations to any research and decision support system. Such a focus requires the development and implementation of a long-range plan for research activities related to enrollment. This focus on enrollment research could also provide assistance in the collection and analysis of data for assessment, strategic planning, program review, accreditation, budgeting, pricing, and trend analysis.

Too often enrollment managers have relied on the excellence of their people and their breadth of experience (and their intuition) to make strategic planning decisions affecting the future of the college. It is certainly not desirable to ignore the important resource that our people are to the strength and future of the college, but there is also a clearly felt need for a more deliberate focus and reliance upon institutional research as another resource to guide us in the years ahead. James Walters, Associate provost and director of admissions at University of North Carolina at Chapel Hill (1994, page 4), reminds us that "classic marketing consists of four basic steps: market research, strategy decisions or positioning, pricing, and promotion. The first, market research, attempts to increase the understanding of client behavior and to establish a base of information for the other three steps of the process." As we consider our roles as enrollment managers, it is important not to skip the "first step" and still expect to be effective in any of the others.

We are in a rapidly changing market. As colleges look to the future, institutional research is essential for institutional effectiveness. More specifically, a college must have an enrollment management research process which collects, manages, and analyzes data and then disseminates the results to support planning and evaluation efforts. Steven Henderson (1993, pages 159-60) suggests several areas to consider in the development of an enrollment research plan:

1. Institutional distinctive identification

2. Program/academic major strengths and weaknesses

3. Market analysis

4. Competitors

5. Enrollment data and yield analysis

6. Financial aid

7. Fiscal analysis

8. Student opinion

Henderson's discussion explores each of these areas in greater detail. The questions that he suggests be answered relating to each area in order to develop "proactive admissions/marketing efforts" would be helpful for the reader to review as well.

The Comprehensive Nature of Enrollment Research

Each college's organizational structure will determine the specific responsibility for certain research areas, but regardless of where the responsibility falls, such an enrollment-focused institutional research process could include the following:

- Student-related studies—such as attrition/retention studies, assessment, institutional performance, and student "fit" studies, graduation rate studies, and demographic profiles.

- Recruitment-related studies—including competition and market analysis, funnel analysis, defining and refining our message and our image, cost/benefit analysis per inquiry source and activity, prospect pool analysis, and enrolled/non-enrolled applicant studies.

- Pricing studies—particularly those related to financial aid and enrollment—including financial aid leveraging matrix, scholarship competitiveness, price sensitivity, and elasticity.

- Develop and maintain a comprehensive database of enrollment-related information for use as a resource for external reporting—assuring the integrity and consistency of reports and surveys that are completed across the institution.

- Design, develop, and distribute internal and external reports relating to recruitment, admissions, enrollment, and retention for undergraduate first-time and transfer students as well as degree completion and graduate students.

- Explore the feasibility of implementing geo-demography as a tool for understanding the market for both traditional and non-traditional students.

- Assist in the research and recommendation of programs to the academic division that would be strategic to reaching the college's enrollment goals.

- Assist in the development of several models to be used in determining enrollment projections that are based on past trends, the current situation, and market research.

- Design and implement research, and provide resulting recommendations, into the college's "secondary" market groups such as churches, schools and parents.

The effective management of a college's enrollment will require an organizational design that assigns specific responsibilities in the area of research and information systems. Such a focus will lead to informed strategic planning, policy-making, and daily decisions. Philip Kotler (1985, pages 48-49) reinforces this theme and points out a frustration that is all too common on many of our campuses today:

> Administrators need appropriate, accessible information in order to make decisions about current and future programs as well as anticipate marketing related problems. Some administrators find the most basic information was never collected or never recorded. In other cases, the information was either sloppily kept or even destroyed. Some educational institutions have collected lots of information but don't know how the information might be usefully organized and interpreted to aid in decision-making.

This "seat-of-the-pants" approach to marketing higher education that results from a lack of research and information is no longer an option in today's ever-changing marketplace. As we work to be good stewards of the resources that God has given to each of our colleges, we must also respond to both qualitative and quantitative research. Such a choice requires a significant investment of time and resources, but assures that we are using those resources most wisely and with the right students.

You cannot use this "seat-of-the-pants" approach and be responsible in the use of donor dollars or tuition revenue in institutional scholarships and financial aid for students. Another area where stewardship of resources is very apparent is in institutional pricing strategies.

6. Manage pricing issues effectively.

Lee Wilcox (1991, page 58), highlights the complexity of the environment for institutional pricing policy development:

> A variety of national trends have converged to cast a spotlight on student financial aid. The decline in high school graduates and resultant competition among colleges, the failure of federal and state financial aid programs to keep pace with college costs, the growing gap between disposable income and college costs, and the increasing difficulty of balancing institutional budgets have each contributed to the increased attention being given to financial aid in enrollment management.

Each of us would agree that the trends that Wilcox identifies are evident on our campuses as well. In fact, we are most likely reminded of these very things daily! Don Hossler (1994, page 28-29) points out that in his consultation with other enrollment managers, "the costs of higher education generated the most concern."

Growth in financial aid programs, particularly in "price discounting" that is institutionally funded, coupled with the increasing percentage of students who are qualifying for such financial aid, makes effective management of pricing issues on any campus of the utmost importance. Consideration of these issues must not be made only by the business officer and financial aid director, but more importantly the issues must be understood and managed by the president, the board, and the president's cabinet in coordination with the enrollment management team. A monograph by Loren Hubbell for the National Association of College and University Business Officers (1992, pages 1-18), cites four policy and operations questions appropriate for such individuals to consider:

- Is discounting necessary to fill the institution with the desired number of students?

- Is the discounting achieving the goal of promoting educational access?

- Is the financial commitment to access supported in other ways throughout the institution, in order to ensure greater success from the investment in diversity?

- Is the financial burden placed on "full-pay" student families too big? Is it appropriate?

Pricing Policy

As Hubbell goes on to point out, "It is important to realize that tuition pricing is influenced by a number of different forces besides financial aid, including rising costs, shortfalls in other revenues, competitive pressure, and opportunity." Broad-based fundamental issues such as these need to be understood by those making pricing decisions. Discounting is a key factor to consider when determining price, but the pricing arena clearly extends into areas beyond the enrollment manager's control. An obvious example of such an area is the increasing presence of governmental regulation and monitoring of higher education, coupled with a decreasing revenue from those sources. The influence of state and federal regulations is felt across a campus, but regulations are perhaps felt most strongly in the area of financial aid administration. Terry Hartle, vice president for governmental relations at the American Council on Education summarizes it this way (1994, page 18):

> Federal aid is a double-edged sword. While essential to the operation of most colleges, this money is sure to beget regulations. Indeed, as the amount of money swells, some federal policy makers see federal aid as leverage that can be used to push universities in certain policy directions. The upshot of increased federal spending is more, and more intrusive, regulations.

Given the complex combination of factors which influence an institution's pricing and financial aid, what then can the enrollment manager do to assure the most effective pricing decisions? First, we can work to be directly involved in decisions like those suggested above. Such discussions will provide a foundation and framework for future decisions and program implementation. Secondly, and certainly as important, we can work to insure a constant and consistent evaluation, review, and monitoring of the institution's financial aid and scholarship programs.

Such a review of financial aid and pricing can come from a variety of sources. Any college using institutionally budgeted scholarship and grant dollars also has the opportunity (and responsibility) to shape and re-shape the policies and practices that distribute those funds. Ongoing, longitudinal research that considers the effectiveness of those programs toward meeting the college's enrollment objectives should evaluate a variety of factors. A review of the external environment would require a close monitoring of the scholarship and financial aid programs of key competitors and peer institutions. Each college should develop its own data set in this area, but several existing sources of research also will be helpful here. The study done by the CCCU which collects and compares various pricing and financial aid factors among the participating colleges provides an excellent source for comparison. In addition, national studies like the "National Enrollment Management Survey" done by Williams Crocket provide another good source of information on a broad range of issues, including pricing and financial aid.

A college's own pricing research can focus on several areas as well. Surveys completed by both enrolling and non-enrolling admitted students each year should ask students to evaluate and compare both need-based and merit-based aid with the other colleges to which they applied. These programs can then be evaluated and adjusted if the research demonstrates that they are not performing as desired. Many colleges are finding that the financial aid leveraging matrix model is another invaluable tool in reviewing and making a more complex analysis of the applicant pool. One commonly used matrix creates a grid which distributes aid applicants according to need levels on one axis and ability levels (G.P.A.) on the other. This type of an analysis can then be used to evaluate yield within targeted sub groups of the population or to compare institutional cost per student and student net cost for each cell within the grid.

Judith Eaton, president of the Council for Aid to Education, points out another "imperative" issue to consider. She states that "the higher education system as currently financed has failed to meet either the needs of the majority of students who are now nontraditional or the needs of the increasing number of students who are academically under- or unprepared." (Eaton, 1993). Certainly this call for restructuring goes well beyond what we can control directly on our campuses, but it is still necessary that each institution look to ways that campus-based programs and the opportunities that we provide can be made available to older, working, part-time, and non-degree students. If serving such students is consistent with our institution's mission, must not we also then look for ways to make our services accessible to them?

Communicating Pricing Issues

On each of our campuses we strive to provide the most excellent educational opportunities possible. And we work to communicate those features and benefits to our customers. But we also struggle more and more with the "value" question. Whether the price growth in higher education is perceived or real, the fact remains that more and more families are feeling priced out of our market. Many of us hear the parents of today's prospective students say, "When we were in college, we were able to work a summer job to pay the next year's tuition. We don't want our child to be burdened with thousands of dollars in debt at graduation." This alone reinforces the critical importance of effectively communicating and addressing college finance issues.

Within the college, staff, faculty, and currents students must be equipped to understand and deal directly with financial aid and related concerns. This is not to say that we must each be financial aid experts, rather the campus must be empowered with the confidence that the enrollment management staff can and will address the details of any situation that may be referred. The careful staffing, structure, and communication by those directly responsible for assisting with college finances on campus is essential to creating a level of satisfaction that reinforces the excellent academic preparation the student is purchasing from the college. Externally these issues become even more apparent. The prospective student must be served in his or her financial concerns by effective and honest publications, timely and accurate events, and a well trained staff. Key to this perspective is a cooperative effort of all individuals and offices involved—particularly the admissions and financial aid offices. How does the administrative organization and campus culture at your college encourage (or discourage) such collaborative efforts?

Our challenge as Christian institutions of higher learning is to not only demonstrate the value of the enterprize of which we are a part, but just as importantly to show integrity and honesty as we work to deal with a confused customer in an ever-changing environment.

7. Respond to new and emerging technologies.

Internet, World Wide Web, Netscape, Mosaic, FTP, URL, Gopher, e-mail, CD-ROM, Home Page, WAIS, PC, Mac, UNIX, HTML, Telnet, NetNews, listserve, Enroll-L, networks, LAN, Windows, DOS, OS/2, modem, http, image management....

Such a list goes on and on and creates an agenda far too long to cover in the space that we have here. And to many of us, the use of such terminology may even sound like a foreign language, but the students that our institutions are serving already see the technology represented by these and other words as part of their world! As enrollment managers, we must carefully consider how we are to get the programs that we manage on track with this technological revolution. The technology train is not slowing down either! In fact it appears to be changing into a supersonic jet! What must we do to get on board?

Technology Versus Stewardship

One of the first issues to be addressed is that of availability of technology vs. stewardship of resources. With the explosion of technological advancements, it is all the more important that we equip ourselves to respond to and use the resources that we have in a stewardly and most effective manner. We need to avoid getting caught in the trap of implementing every new idea that comes along, but we must also work to demonstrate that our institutions are not blind to the world in which we are preparing our students to serve. Such a thoughtful, campus-wide response to technology can serve as a foundation to explore opportunities that a college or university could effectively use in the implementation of these resources in enrollment management and throughout the campus.

Student Records

One of the foundational areas where the effective use of technology needs to be addressed on every campus is that of administrative student records software. The development of either an in-house or purchased software program that can provide an integrated campus-wide student data base is essential. Records on past, present, and future students must provide for data that is reliable, retrievable, usable, and understandable. Student records systems that directly affect enrollment should allow for individualized tracking of student contacts throughout the entire "admissions funnel." They must also provide for accurate, up-to-date reporting and personalized, tailored, and timely responses to inquiries. Using a well-developed prospective student data base can also be very effective in qualifying and "grading" the prospect pool in order to most efficiently target the markets that are most appropriate for our institution. Certainly this shopping list can go on and on, but the fundamental issue here is assurance that we are collecting and then able to use information most effectively as we market our institution.

The shopping list of other areas to consider is expanding daily, but below are some that seem to merit consideration. Many colleges and universities are using these to some degree or another. What options should we be considering?

The Internet

Educational institutions have had connections via the Internet for 25 years, but recent developments have made Internet a household word even beyond academia. And this trend gives every indication it is going to continue. A "web site" detailing the history of the Internet claims that the Internet is growing at a rate of 160 percent per year, is connected to 149 e-mail countries, and has more than three million computer lines to the system. High schools, businesses, government, and even homes via on-line services all are rapidly joining colleges and universities on the Internet. The wealth of information through this medium is enormous, and one could easily get buried and overwhelmed by it all. Enrollment managers should consider a few aspects of the Internet that appear to be very important as we work to reach the students of the next century:

E-mail—Many of us know the Internet most directly because of our use of e-mail. Electronic mail that leaves our campus uses the Internet. Listing your e-mail address on your business card is becoming almost as commonplace as a phone number—and in many ways a more efficient means of communication. This, for no other reason, could be a strong motivation for establishing an e-mail address for your admissions office. Students inquiring via an admissions@your.institution.edu e-mail address that is provided in publications and on letterhead could receive an immediate response to their e-mail address along with any more detailed reply via "snail mail" or telephone. E-mail access is especially convenient when working with students who are overseas with limited access to expensive telephone systems and inefficient mail delivery. E-mail is also a very effective way to communicate with colleagues at your own or at other institutions.

Discussion Groups via E-mail—There are hundreds of "discussion groups" organized around various topics that use what is called a "listserve" to distribute a single message to an entire list of individual e-mail addresses. These provide a forum to share ideas, ask questions, and seek out the resources and expertise of others with similar interest. Some discussion groups that relate closely to enrollment management are:

- ENROLL-L "The AACRAO/NASPA Enrollment Management Exchange" To subscribe, send the following message to: LISTSERV@VM1.SPCS.UMN.EDU
  SUBSCRIBE ENROLL-L Your Name

- FINAID-L "A forum for discussion of matters related to the administration of financial aid." To subscribe, send the following message to: LISTSERV@PSUVM.PSU.EDU
  SUBSCRIBE FINAID-L Your Name

- REGIST-L "Registrar discussion list" To subscribe, send the following message to: LISTSERV@GSUVM1.GSU.EDU
  SUBSCRIBE REGIST-L Your Name

Any individual with an e-mail address may subscribe to such a list and then receive and send mail to the other list members. Subscribing to these lists is a simple process and the listserve will respond with further details regarding the list once your request is received. Not everything that is discussed on these lists is relevant to each individual's situation, but a quick review of the subjects of the posted messages will allow you to select and review those that are of interest. These discussions are another helpful way to be aware of today's current topic in your field and to share in the wisdom of your colleagues. Perhaps those of us working in enrollment management at Christian colleges will choose to develop an "electronic discussion group" that would allow us to continue sharing the types of ideas that we are sharing in this publication!

World Wide Web—The web or WWW is exploding with resources and web sites that provide multimedia presentations of information on an unbelievably wide range of subjects. Using browsers (such as Netscape or Mosaic) that can display both text and graphics, many colleges and universities have already created home pages where their institution can be located on the web using an URL (Universal Resource Locator) that points the user to their site on the web. There even have been a few enterprising businesses, including Peterson's "Internet Education Center," that have developed web pages that allow students to do a college search by filling in a form on their web page. The student is then directed to the home pages of those colleges that match the entered profile. From there students can view more detailed information, see photos, tour the campus via an interactive map, and even submit an inquiry or application for admission electronically. Although high schools and homes are just beginning to have greater access to the web, by every appearance this seems to be the way to communicate with tomorrow's students. Two web pages that provide links to the home pages of colleges and universities throughout the world can be found at the following URLs:

- *American and International Universities*:
  http://www.mit.edu.8001/people/cdmello/univ.html
- *American Universities Only*:
  http://www.clas.ufl.edu/CLAS/american-universities.html

Reviewing examples from these sites will help each of our institutions to begin making sure that our home page presents our institution in an accurate and helpful way. Your college's catalog, course schedule, and even registration itself may soon be commonplace on the web!

Technology and Communication with Students

Beyond the Internet, several other technological developments merit our consideration. With the advent of CD-ROM technology and the presence of computers in the homes and schools of many of our prospective students, we need to also consider if the 30-page paper viewbook of today needs to become the electronically stored publication of tomorrow. The same can be said for application forms. Many colleges currently offer the option of submitting an application via floppy disk. Each new medium such as this deserves our careful consideration, but one drawback of storing these publications on disk is that they become out of date almost as soon as they are produced. One wonders, though, if our admissions home page on the web will become the most effective viewbook of tomorrow, since the information contained there can be updated daily if need be—for little or no cost!

Remember when the college with a video seemed to be on the cutting edge? What place does video have in our enrollment management tool kit today? Is it the technology of yesterday? Are videos effective and worth the expense? Are they outdated shortly after they are produced? These questions beg for more space than we have here, but if nothing else they reinforce the need to carefully evaluate each new technological medium that comes along—and then to re-evaluate on an ongoing basis.

Our campuses also have a responsibility to serve our current students in the uses of technology. Thomas DeLoughry, in the February 24, 1995, issue of **The Chronicle of Higher Education** (pages A25-A26) describes "electronic information kiosks" as something that "many college officials hope will become as popular with students as automatic teller machines become with bank customers." The article goes on to explain that:

> The kiosks are being used to offer visitors videotaped welcome messages from top administrators, computerized campus maps, faculty and student directories, lists of coming events, and other services. On many campuses,...students can retrieve their financial aid records, grades, or class schedules for the upcoming semester.

Whether our institution chooses to put its viewbook on CD-ROM, automate its library, or simply put the director of admissions' photo on the Internet, we must work to develop an appropriate response to technology and acknowledge its impact on enrollment. Regardless of how we answer the questions that these issues raise, we must have an institutional commitment to make appropriate use of technology, make wise choices as to how to keep the pace and still afford the cost, and then provide these services for our students. As enrollment managers let's work to ask the questions that could get our colleges on that supersonic jet before it leaves the runway!

As the science of enrollment management increases in complexity, leaders in higher education must also remain vigilant in defining sound ethical parameters. Technology presents us with many new opportunities to interact with students, but we must be sure that these and any other contacts that we have be done with integrity.

8. Commit to integrity and ethical behavior.

Doing things right or doing the right thing—is there a difference? As the competitive pressure increases and presidents and boards of trustees become anxious about enrollment goals, the ethical framework that characterized enrollment management for the past 20 years is in jeopardy. From the mid-1970s until the late 1980s, the ethical questions of enrollment management were related to recruitment and marketing practices (i.e. truth in advertising questions), and to a lesser degree, financial aid distribution and merit scholarships. The enrollment management environment, such as it was in those years, was regulated by the National Association of College Admissions Counselors (NACAC) Statement of Principles of Good Practice. During the 1980s, the National Association of Christian College Admissions Personnel (NACCAP) grew as an important organization influencing Christian liberal arts and Bible colleges. Interestingly, NACCAP struggled with adopting and policing a statement of good practice.

An Environment of Concern and an Opportunity for Leadership

That struggle to adopt a statement of good practice was hard to understand. Why did so many NACCAP members find it difficult to endorse either the NACAC statement or one of their own? There seemed to be an ends-justify-the-means mentality when the end was defined as building God's Kingdom. There were many NACCAP meetings during the 1980s when one member college accused another of stealing their prospects by deceiving presentations about what opportunities were or were not available. Many member schools were struggling to meet enrollment goals and accused those colleges whose enrollment situation was more secure of failing to understand competitive pressures. Thus, for many years, Christian colleges were lumped together with other secular fringe institutions as mavericks in following ethical guidelines. A poor witness at best!

Fortunately, as the competition for students has increased in the recent past, NACCAP has an approved "Statement of Good Practices" and has worked hard to teach member institutions what their responsibilities are. This developmental process is an admirable act of leadership by key individuals within NACCAP and merits the thanks of anyone caring about the witness of the church in today's society. Unfortunately, the development of such a statement is necessary because the long-held definitions of good practice are threatened. It is a time when Christian leaders in higher education have a unique opportunity to communicate a basis for ethical behavior that has as its central premise the Lordship of Christ.

A Basis for Ethical Practices in Enrollment Management

In John 17:20-24, Jesus prays for all believers—that "all of them might be one." This oneness that Jesus has with the Father and we with him is an image of how we as Christian college enrollment managers might consider our marketing practices and the ethics of our behaviors. If we are one in our sense of mission to Christ's lordship, we are obedient so that "...the world may believe that you have sent me." We must work tirelessly to present a clear message in the marketplace that our enrollment management behaviors are based on our oneness in Christ.

Character formation is one of the shared goals of Christian higher education. Institutions ought to consider that this modeling of Christian behavior begins in our interactions with prospective students. Thus, statements about our institutions that were not completely honest or financial aid awards that manipulated the decision-making of a family have no place in our enrollment management plans. Mark Schwehn, in his recent book **Exiles from Eden** (1993) calls higher education to return to an environment of virtue, charity, self-denial, and trust. He contends that if inquiry is an activity carried out in community, progress will depend on the presence of these virtues. Since enrollment management is an activity involving the whole institution, we must consider the implications of Schwehn's reminder. Perhaps a discussion about these implications with representatives of departments and divisions involved in enrollment management would be a most beneficial activity.

"Spiritual traits" of an Enrollment Management Program

Dr. Richard Mouw, president of Fuller Theological Seminary, in a speech reflecting on Schwehn's thesis and the responsibility of institutions of higher learning, said there are certain "spiritual traits" that institutions must nurture in students. These spiritual traits also provide a basis for institutional administrative life:

1. *Integrity*: We desire our students to be "integrated people," holding together in our faith in Christ as expressed in Colossians 1.

2. *Academic friendship*: Open yourself up to God and then to others. Live with a spirit of servanthood.

3. *Humility*: Campuses often are more accurately described as places of arrogance and need for personal achievement. We could better assume a posture of "cognitive humility."

4. *Patience*: Mouw has a chapter in his recent book **Uncommon Decency** (1992, page 157) entitled "Serving a Slow God." This follows a chapter reflecting on the long-suffering ministry of Mother Teresa. Mouw points

out that flexibility, tentativeness, humility, awe, and modesty are traits we develop in sharing in God's patience.

Nothing is more important than enrollment managers doing their work as models of servanthood. Unfortunately, we know several colleagues who had to resign from their position of leadership (most often directors of admission) because the bottom line enrollment goal was more important than representing the institution with integrity. Presidents and boards of trustees need to hear from thoughtful enrollment managers about what is at stake if they fail to encourage ethical practices, thoughtful planning and organization, and effective team-work across the campus. Our oneness in Christ must be demonstrated in every activity and by each individual across all of our campuses—let's be sure it begins with us as enrollment managers.

RESOURCES

American Council on Higher Education. Thirteenth Annual Status Report Minorities in Higher Education. Washington, DC: American Council on Education, 1994.

Association of Governing Boards of Universities and Colleges. **Trustees and Troubled Times in Higher Education**. Washington, D.C.: Association of Governing Boards of Universities and Colleges, 1992.

Baldridge, Victor, and Deal, Terence. **The Dynamics of Organizational Change in Education**. Berkley: McCutchen Publishing Co., 1983.

Cohen, M. D. and Marsh, J.G. **Leadership and Ambiguity: The American College President**. New York: MacGraw-Hill, 1974.

DeLoughry, Thomas J. "Computerized Kiosks: Electronic units assist visitors and give students easy access to their records." **The Chronicle of Higher Education**, February 24, 1995.

DePree, Max. **Leadership is an Art**. New York: Doubleday, 1989.

Dolence, M. **Strategic Enrollment Management: A Primer For Campus Administrators**. American Association of Collegiate Registrars and Admissions Officers (AACRAO) and Datatel, Inc. 1993.

Drucker, Peter. "Management and the Role of the Worker," **Harvard Business Review**, September-October 1988.

Glover, R. H., "Designing a Decision-Support System for Enrollment Management." **Research in Higher Education**. Vol. 24, No. 1, 1986.

Graff, Steven. **New Directions in Higher Education**, "Organizing the Resources That Can be Effective," March 1986.

Gratz, Robert, and Salem, Philip. **Organizational Communication and Higher Education**, AAHE-ERIC/Higher Education Research Report No. 10, Washington, D.C.: American Council on Education, 1988.

Greenleaf, Robert. **Servant Leadership: A Journey into the Nature of Legitimate Power and Greatness**. New York: Paulist Press, 1977.

Hartle, T. "The Battle over Regulation of Academe." **The College Board Review**, No. 172, Summer 1994.

Henderson, Steven J., "Cost-effective Enrollment Management: A Cornerstone of Institutional Advancement." **Winning Strategies in Challenging Times for Advancing Small Colleges**. Council for the Advancement and Support of Education, 1993.

Hodgkinson, Harold. **Independent Higher Education in a Nation of Nations**. Washington, DC: National Institute of Independent Colleges and Universities, 1993.

Hossler, D. "Enrollment Management in the 1990s." **The Admissions Strategist**. No. 20, Spring 1994. The College Board, New York, NY.

Hossler, Donald. **Creating Effective Enrollment Management Systems**. New York: The College Board, 1986.

Hossler, Donald. **Enrollment Management: An Integrated Approach**. New York: The College Board, 1984.

Hubbell, Lauren-Loomis. **Tuition Discounting: The Impact of Institutionally Funded Financial Aid**. National Association of College and University Business Officers. Washington, D.C., 1992.

Institute of International Education. **Open Doors**, 1993-1994. New York: Annual Report of the Institute of International Education.

Katzenbach, Jon and Smith, Douglas. "The Discipline of Teams," **Harvard Business Review**. March-April 1993.

Keller, G. **Academic Strategy: The Management Revolution in American Higher Education**. Baltimore, MD: Johns Hopkins University Press, 1983.

Keller, G. "Strategic Planning and Management in a Competitive Environment." In R. Glover and M. Krotseng (eds.), **Developing Executive Information Systems for Higher Education**. New Directions in Institutional Research, no. 77. San Francisco: Jossey-Bass Inc., 1993.

Kemmerer, Frank et al. **Strategies for Effective Enrollment Management**. Washington, DC: American Association of State Colleges and Universities, 1982.

Kotler, Philip and Fox, Karen F. A., **Strategic Marketing for Educational Institutions**. Englewood Cliffs, NJ: Prentice-Hall, Inc., 1985.

Mac Donald, Mary Jane, "Never a Dull Moment at Denison," **CASE Currents**, February 1994.

Mortensen, Thomas G. **Postsecondary Education Opportunity**. Iowa City: a monthly newsletter.

Mouw, Richard. **Uncommon Decency**. Downers Grove, IL: InterVarsity Press, 1992 .

Peters, Tom and Waterman, Robert. **In Search of Excellence**. New York: Warner Books, 1982.

Schwehn, Mark. **Exiles From Eden**. New York, NY: Oxford University Press, 1993.

Walters, James C., "Market Research—The First Step in Your Marketing Program." **College & University**, Vol. LXX, No. 1, Fall 1994.

Western Interstate Commission of the States. High School Graduates Projections by State 1992-2009. Boulder: Western Interstate Commission of the States, 1993.

Wilcox, L. "Evaluating the Impact of Financial Aid," In D. Hossler (ed.), **Evaluating Student Recruitment and Retention Programs. New Directions in Institutional Research**, No 70. San Francisco: Jossey-Bass Inc., 1991.

About the Authors

PETER HARKEMA is vice president for student life and enrollment services at Fuller Theological Seminary in Pasadena, California. Peter spent 21 years in enrollment management related positions at Calvin College before beginning at Fuller in August 1995. He was awarded Admissions Officer of the Year in 1988 by National Association of Christian College Admissions Personnel. He is a Calvin graduate of 1971, received an M.A. in college personnel and counseling from Western Michigan University in 1981 and a Ph.D. in college and university administration from Michigan State University in 1990. Pete's wife Jill is an administrator with the Salvation Army, their daughter Dawn is a student at Calvin, and their other children, Peter and Anna, are in high school and elementary school respectively.

DALE KUIPER serves as director of enrollment research at Calvin College. In addition to his research responsibilities for the enrollment services division, he also has management responsibilities within the admissions office. He has worked at Calvin 14 years on the residence life, admissions, and financial aid staffs. Dale was elected to the executive committee of the National Association of Christian College Admissions Personnel for four years and was awarded a NACCAP Regional Service Award in 1994. Dale earned a master's degree in management from Aquinas College in 1991. He and his wife Esther, a community education director for the Grand Rapids Public Schools, have two children, Kyle and Kelsey.

Chapter 6

Public Relations in Advancement: Targeting for Results

JOHN L. GLANCY

*C**lutching her leather briefcase, public relations director Jan Target entered the expansive office.*

"Come in, Jan," boomed the voice of Hopeful College's newly appointed president, Dr. William Goal. A former business school dean, Goal was known for his bottom line management style.

"Here, sit down," he said, motioning Target to a chair. "Now tell me, what's going on in your shop?"

"Well Dr. Goal, we've already sent out 30 press releases this week, and it's only Wednesday. In fact, I brought along this report that shows how much our publicity would have cost at normal advertising rates. But we got it all free."

"I see," said Goal, pulling his reading glasses from his pocket and eyeing the document.

"I've also been visiting all our sponsoring churches," Target continued. "It's great just chatting with the pastors. And wait until you see our new admissions viewbook. My wife and kids are my toughest critics and they think it's great."

Goal sighed, laid down his glasses and slowly began to speak, "Jan, I know God can work in mysterious ways, but let me explain how I want us to go about our public relations efforts from now on ..."

Public Relations for Christian Higher Education

The fictitious "Ms. Target" is just about to get a crash course in current public relations thought. Up to now, her efforts have focused more on process than on outcomes. Today, public relations thinking is honing in on the end product more than the process. Rayburn and Preston writing in **CASE Currents** put it bluntly.

> The days of the warm fuzzies in public relations are over. News releases merely for publicity—finished. Newsletter after newsletter just to keep alumni informed—done. Bonuses based only on column inches of newsprint—gone! (1990, page 27).

Christian higher education has not escaped this economic squeeze. We struggle with the same issues as public institutions. But is fiscal accountability the only reason we strive to bolster the bottom line? Should our approach be different from secular education? In their book, **Strategy for Leadership**, Ed Dayton and Ted Engstrom offer principles that can be adapted to our roles as public relations professionals within Christian higher education (1979, pages 32-33).

1. **We are working to fulfill God's purposes on earth.** The news releases, publications, special events, and other public relations activities take on a new meaning when we see them as means to an eternal end. By indirectly influencing the lives of students on campus, we're helping prepare them to carry out God's purposes throughout the world.

2. **We measure all our efforts in terms of biblical values and principles.** Our public relations efforts should always be characterized by truth, honesty, righteousness, fair play, etc. This is not to say other schools can't have high values, too, but ours are a given—a biblical plumbline to which all efforts are measured.

3. **We have assurance that the ultimate purpose for which we're working will one day be recognized.** The seeds we sow now in the lives of our students will reap eternal rewards at the Lord's return. As Paul told the Christians at Corinth, "...you are a letter from Christ, the result of our ministry, written not with ink but with the Spirit of the living God, not on tablets of stone but on tablets of human hearts." (II Cor. 3:3).

In addition, we in Christian higher education are called to be accountable. As Larry Burkett puts it, "without a system of checks and balances, anyone will eventually drift off course" (Burkett, 1990, page 18). In the Lord's parable of the talents, the master called his servants to account for their actions. Those who showed good stewardship were commended. For those in Christian higher education, limited resources demand responsible stewardship; an emphasis on results-oriented, strategic public relations planning is not only commendable but a necessity.

In short, all public relations efforts in Christian higher education can be summed up in Christ's words in Matthew 5:16: "Let your light so shine before men that they may see your good works and glorify your Father in heaven." Whether its producing a viewbook, writing a speech, or promoting a program, our aim should be toward excellence for the glory of God. That's the charge that should set all our public relations strategies in motion.

Defining Marketing and PR

Results-oriented public relations includes increased use of marketing theory. The term "marketing" encompasses all the activities necessary to move a product (education) from manufacturer (college) to consumer (student). This involves product research, product development, branding, pricing, packaging, transporta-

118

tion, sales and distribution, advertising, and public relations (Reilly, 1981, page 319).

Public relations, then, is an element of the total marketing effort. Informally defined, public relations includes generating publicity, strategizing, creating political awareness, managing a communication network, building internal and community relations, and a variety of other activities from fact-finding to program evaluation (Reilly, 1981, page 6).

Robert Topor, in **Marketing Higher Education**, suggests that higher education should approach marketing and public relations as integrated activities. A planned promotional program for a college assigns each department or subunit appropriate goals which are reinforced by the institution's total public relations plan. This plan is comprehensive and includes opportunities for promotion of the larger unit, as well as the individual subunits (1983, page 6).

For example, the admissions office has its own target populations, the development office has its own constituencies, and the music department that sends out the college choir to churches and schools has its distinct audiences. Although there is overlap in the target audiences, each of these institutional subunits, which has its own set of goals, can reinforce the other and ultimately build the reputation and image of the college as a whole.

Integrated Marketing Communications

An emerging model for marketing communications that directly impacts public relations activities is the concept of integrated marketing communications or IMC. The IMC model organizes all messages communicated by an institution and attempts to integrate them to achieve successful communication results.

Sandra Moriarty, writing in **Public Relations Quarterly**, notes that "every contact point that a stakeholder has with an organization is a communications opportunity" (1994, page 38). These "opportunities" come in both planned and unplanned varieties. She cites four types of messages relating to the IMC model: a) planned messages (e.g. printed publications, news releases, etc.); b) inferred messages (e.g. impressions gained by prospects after a campus visit, campus neighbors views of college parking policies, etc.); c) maintenance messages (e.g. day-to-day interaction between campus employees and prospects, donors, callers, etc.); and d) unplanned messages (e.g. calls from reporters, student protests, etc.) (1994, pages 38-39).

In reality, the management or influencing of these messages is often the responsibility of more than one person or office. Perhaps a cross-campus team approach, led by the public relations office, is the most realistic way of managing the communications process. The goal of this effort would be to integrate institutional messages to form an effective "synergy" of communication. In this sense, message synergy "means that various messages, if they are coordinated and consistent, add up to communication with more impact than any of the individual messages can create by themselves" (Moriarty, 1994, page 40).

Components of Message Integration

Moriarty cites work by her colleague Tom Duncan at the University of Colorado regarding a model of how messages are integrated. The three components of this message integration model as they relate to college advancement activities include the following.

1. **Consistency.** Research shows that people integrate messages naturally. All the different message fragments they receive (campus viewbook, homecoming flyer, newspaper ad, etc.) fit together to form an overall impression of an institution. An image that holds together is one whose various communication components are saying the same thing. Without that kind of consistency, the image inevitably will be fuzzy.

2. **Interactivity.** This component focuses on using computer database software to segment a mass audience into more manageable populations and then create communication programs that promote dialog. Databases and new media technologies, currently emerging, will make it possible to move to a more personal two-way communication system.

3. **Mission.** The final component of synergistic communication involves mission marketing or the idea that the institution stands for something beyond its end product, financial health, or endowment. The organization's mission, or reason for existence, becomes a fundamental component of all institutional communication (1994, page 41).

In Christian higher education, striving for consistent messages in communications and finding new interactive ways to connect with constituents will be important to our overall advancement efforts. But the ultimate goal, and opportunity, is the communication of our mission as Christian institutions, that is, impacting the world for God through the lives of our students, faculty and staff, and graduates.

Whatever marketing theory or public relations techniques we use, they should not be a substitute for the leading of God. Larry Johnston, writing in **Money for Ministries**, talks about "marketing-burned" organizations. These organizations have been so driven by marketing programs and principles that they've lost sight of who's ultimately in control. "We see reliance on methods replacing reliance on the Maker, and reliance on technique replacing reliance on the Holy Spirit. These organizations have become so accustomed to what works that they have forgotten who does the work: 'Unless the Lord builds the house, its builders labor in vain' (Psalm 127:1)" (1989, page 241).

Public Relations Planning

Jan Target swiveled around in her chair and picked up the ringing phone.

"Hello, Target here."

"Hi Jan, this is Rich," said Hopeful's Alumni Director Richard Class.

"Yes, Rich, what can I do for you?"

"Well, we just had an alumni board meeting and came up with a great idea. We want to have an alumni missions conference this summer on campus. We'll

*bring in alumni missionaries from all over the country—the world! We're hav-
ing another meeting in three days to discuss details and I need you to put a promotional plan together for me. What do you say?"*

"Sure, Rich, I'll come up with something. Talk to you soon."

Target no sooner cradled the receiver than the phone rang again.

*"Jan, this is Roger," said the voice of Target's boss, vice president Roger
Forward. "Remember that dinner for major contributors to the Chapel fund?
Well, we had to move it up a month. We'll need the invitations that much sooner.
Plus, I'd like you to research some background material we'll use to honor a few
special contributors. Keep me informed. Thanks."*

"Yes...you're welcome," mumbled Target, hanging up the phone.

*"Hi Jan," said Target's assistant Debbie as she walked into the office. "I
just got back from a meeting with the admissions people. They want brochures to
describe all of our 44 majors and they want them for fall travel this year."*

*Target's glazed eyes fell to some papers on her desk. Her stare fixed on a
memo from the campus chaplain. Three faith and learning symposiums were
being planned with nationally known speakers. Would she coordinate publicity?*

*Pulling open her desk drawer, Target pushed aside the paper clips and
reached for the Excedrin bottle. "Ugh," she groaned, "Where do I start?"*

How often have we, like Jan Target, been caught in a priority squeeze? As requests come in, we say yes to them all because with no prioritization scheme, all
have equal priority.

And how often are we forced into working nights, weekends, etc., to accomplish those "impossible" demands? We're caught focusing on the "what" of the
assignment, where activity equates to accomplishment. However, our vision
should be elsewhere, says consultant Kalman B. Druck: "As long as advancement
officers think they're hired to write news releases, run alumni meetings, put out
publications, and so on, they'll never consider why they do these things" (1988,
page 3).

Examining the "why" of activities takes us away from concentrating solely on
means and looks to the end. We must ask ourselves, "Are we accomplishing our
institutional objectives or simply engaging in legitimate but unfocused activities?"

Institutional Strategic Planning

Ideally, advancement professionals will be able to use the institution's strategic
plan as a road map for public relations efforts. However, what if your college or
university doesn't have such a plan?

Hopefully, the public relations office can help generate one. Susan Bonnet, a
past advancement contributor to **CASE Currents**, offers some overall guidelines
on what should be included in an institutional strategic plan: 1) define your institution's mission, 2) scan the environment and identify your institution's unique
challenges and opportunities, 3) assess your institution's strengths and weaknesses, 4) set priorities, and 5) outline strategies for achieving goals (1988, pages
4-5).

Druck says that an ideal PR plan should first fit into an overall institutional plan. That is, the ideal PR plan will seek to produce tangible results to meet institutional goals. Second, it will support the other advancement areas in your institution. Specific tailored plans for alumni relations, development, admissions, church relations, etc. will all be included. Therefore, the PR plan is an umbrella that covers departmental/area plans and provides the public relations goals to support them (1988, page 3).

To illustrate typical institutional goals within Christian higher education, we can look at research gained from a survey of Coalition for Christian Colleges & Universities member institutions. The initial 1985 survey dealt with a variety of advancement topics and concerns and was later updated in 1989 and 1994, providing a basis for comparison. By looking at the "1" position on the "Very Important" scale in Table 6-1, we can list the three most important institutional public relations goals identified by CCCU institutions in 1994 as: 1) attracting prospective students (85 percent), 2) building and holding goodwill for the institution (67.1 percent), and 3) adding to the college's academic reputation (54.2 percent). The goal of raising funds was a close fourth (52.1 percent). This picture was essentially the same in 1989, with a focus on the college's academic reputation trading places with raising funds.

Table 6-1
Public Relations Goals of Institution (frequency count)

Public Relations Goals	Very Important			of Little Importance		
	1	2	3	4	5	6
Attracting prospective students	61	9	1	1	0	0
Building and holding good will for the institution	49	13	6	1	2	0
Adding to the college's academic reputation	39	20	8	3	1	1
Raising funds	38	16	14	3	1	1
Encouraging favorable community relations	31	26	9	4	1	1
Showing the importance of religion in education	16	25	16	9	2	3
Reporting news	14	24	18	10	3	2
Encouraging favorable relations with faculty	11	18	27	5	6	3
Educating the public about higher education	6	14	18	15	11	4
Providing a community service	4	16	25	13	8	1

Categories that moved a positive seven percentage points or more from 1989 to 1994 were: promoting favorable community relations (12.1 percent), attracting prospective students (11 percent), enhancing faculty relations (8.3 percent), enhancing the college's reputation (7.2 percent), and building goodwill (7.1 percent). The category of showing importance of religion in education dropped from 45 percent in 1985 to 28 percent in 1989 and 22.5 percent in 1994. The least important goal in all three studies was educating the public about higher education.

Elements of a PR Plan

There are many variations on the theme of what should be included in a public relations plan. The following outline is based on one used by Thomas Harrison (Harrison, 1990, Notes). A PR plan should include:

1. **A Situation Analysis.** Examine your school's mission statement, direction, competition, and circumstances of operation.

2. **A Statement of Goals.** Include a handful of qualitative statements that support your institutional mission and identify the key priority items (e.g. seek the highest quality Christian liberal arts faculty, etc.).

3. **A Statement of Objectives.** Ideally these items should be drawn from your institution's overall strategic plan and be very specific and measurable, e.g. what kind of students you want to attract, how much money for the annual fund, etc.

4. **A Series of Strategies.** Develop statements that tell how you plan to reach your objectives.

5. **A Listing of Tactics.** For each strategy, there should be a list of nitty gritty tactics of how the strategy will be accomplished. For example, if publicity is the strategy for a specific program or event, then the tactics would include media relations, press kits, news releases, etc.

6. **Designated Target Audiences.** Alumni, faculty, prospective students, donors, churches, parents, etc.

7. **Appropriate Target Messages.** This is the place to set the theme of your entire communications program.

8. **Desired Target Media.** Publications, publicity, advertising, personal contact, etc.

9. **A Time Table.** Beginning and end of program.

10. **Required Staffing.**

11. **Budget Parameters.**

12. **A Process for Evaluation.** Upon each project's completion, evaluate how close you came to meeting your objectives. Make this a formal, ongoing process to help you "course correct" whenever needed.

Creating a public relations plan frees you from the constant reactive status of fulfilling everyone's request every time. The plan should define your priorities and give direction to your efforts.

One thing deserves emphasizing. Don't develop your plan in isolation. Include your staff and especially your supervisor(s). To free you from the "priority squeeze," your plan must be endorsed by higher administration and ideally the president. Then you have a framework for your day-to-day activities.

Take Time for Research

"I want to know what our constituencies think about us," said Hopeful College's Vice President Roger Forward as he surveyed his advancement team around the conference room table. "What about prospective students?"

"Overall, they see us as a bit restrictive," said Mary Roads, director of admissions. "They think we're tied up in rules. And lots of them confuse us with the seminary down the road."

"Hmmm," said Forward. "How about you, Tony?"

Church Relations Director Anthony Pew responded, ."We've really got two groups, Roger. The old guard pastors think we're teaching liberal theology. That's balanced by the young pastors fresh out of seminary. They think we're right on."

"I call on a lot of people," interjected Cash Crowley, director of development. "Too many don't know much about us at all. That's a mystery to me."

Forward turned to PR Director Jan Target. "What about your area, Jan. How do the media see us?"

"Well, they only remember the past, like we're still a sleepy little religious school out in the country."

"But we've got 1,600 students and 35 majors!" Forward protested.

"I know," said Target, "but try and tell them that."

"O.K.," said Forward, "I think we've got an image problem. What are we going to do about it?"

This is Jan Target's golden opportunity to reach into her briefcase and pull out a proposal for a research project. She should eloquently argue that even though her colleagues' opinions are valuable, they are not solely the basis on which to build a communications plan. To really determine what Hopeful's constituencies perceive, they need to be systematically asked.

Marketing research should be a vital part of the public relations plan. Among the Coalition for Christian Colleges & Universities members surveyed in 1994, 35 percent indicated they had done a readership survey of their primary institutional publication within the last three years. While these institutions are to be commended, too often such research never gets implemented. Usually it's because of no money, or time constraints, or lack of expertise. Decisions are then made based on perceptions rather than reliable data. Smaller institutions with limited budgets should not reject research out of hand because research doesn't have to be expensive to be effective. Business faculty members and/or marketing classes are a good source for survey development and implementation. CASE (Washington DC) also carries a variety of resource materials to help in the research process.

Topor gives a helpful definition of market research and its primary purpose for educational institutions:

> Market research is any kind of research that gives you informa-
> tion about the current state of your particular market and offers
> guidance in improving your position in that market. In most cases,
> it will involve opinion research, employing scientific sampling and
> interviews or written questionnaires. Educational institutions most
> often use market research as a way to (1) increase the effective-
> ness of their fundraising efforts, or (2) attract more (or better)
> students. Even image studies or projects are usually tied to one of
> these goals (1983, page 29).

Constituents can look at your institution in three ways. First, they can like you. Second, they may not like you, and, third, they may not even know you exist. To create and/or maintain a positive image in the minds of your constituents is a continuing process for advancement officers.

Public relations specialist Andy Marken defines corporate image as the perceived sum of the entire organization, its objectives, and plans. Corporate image encompasses the company's products, services, management style, communications activities and actions around the world (1990, page 21). Everything about an organization talks, says Topor. Items that may add to (or detract from?) the image of your institution include everything from employees to publications to physical plant to the logos painted on maintenance vehicles (1983, page 89). Or, as Robert Sevier puts it writing in **CASE Currents**, "...strong images don't just happen. They require detailed planning and execution. Images must be managed" (1994, page 49).

The ultimate goal of image research is developing communication strategies to reinforce or alter an existing image. Formal research can be conducted to determine how your institution is currently perceived within your target audience(s). With these results in hand, you can fine tune or overhaul, as the case may be, what you want your image to be. However, whatever is projected should be based in fact.

Marken offers five steps that should precede launching a corporate image communications program: 1) evaluate strengths and weaknesses of your institution's current image, 2) define the image that your institution wants to project, 3) determine a course of action that appeals to the largest number of your target audience, 4) create audience-specific selling themes (make certain each selling theme is compatible and in line with the overall image theme), and 5) coordinate every channel of communications to build the desired image (1990, page 22).

In response to the 1994 Coalition for Christian Colleges & Universities questionnaire, institutions felt the following were responsible for modifying image: the president (43.7 percent), the board of trustees (9.9 percent), the advancement office (28.2 percent), and all of the above plus others such as the student development office and faculty (18.3 percent).

Member institutions that responded were split almost down the middle as to whether they were satisfied with their image or felt it needed adjustment. In responding to the statement, "I think that our image(s) should be modified to more adequately satisfy the needs of our clientele," the responses indicated that: 6.9 percent "strongly agreed," 19.4 percent "moderately agreed," 16.7 percent "slightly agreed," while 12.5 percent "slightly disagreed," 30.5 moderately disagreed,"and 13.9 percent "strongly disagreed."

The CCCU institutions were asked to prioritize the kind of image they were trying to project. The table below displays the responses. The strongest attributes of image were Christian character and academic excellence.

Table 6-2
Institutional Image (frequency count)

Image Goal	Very Important				of Little Importance			
	1	2	3	4	5	6	7	8
Christian character	45	18	1	3	1	0	0	0
Academic excellence	28	28	8	1	4	0	0	0
Teaching quality	5	15	30	12	4	1	1	0
Fiscal stability	1	6	10	17	10	15	8	1
Service to the church	2	6	10	17	19	11	2	1
Community service	1	3	9	5	16	15	14	5
Faculty research	0	2	2	2	4	3	8	46
Christian occupations of alumni	0	4	1	4	6	16	29	8

In comparing the 1989 and 1994 surveys, the ranking of image goal items (e.g. Christian character, etc.) remained essentially the same. However, almost all the percentages in the number "1" position on the "of great importance" scale dropped from 1989 to 1994. For example, "Teaching quality" fell 14.6 percent, "Quality academics" 11.4 percent, "Service to church" 7.1 percent, and "Christian character" 5.8 percent. This trend still holds true when analyzing position points "1" and "2" on the "of great importance" scale. However, "Christian character" remained virtually even.

It is important to note that an institution's ability to communicate a favorable image to its many publics places it in a position to reap many benefits in terms of funds, friends, and freshmen. Or, as Solomon put it in Proverbs 22:1, "A good name is more desirable than great riches; to be esteemed is better than silver or gold." Although people act (or don't act) on the basis of image, it must be grounded in substance, for as Marken concludes, "A sound corporate image is no substitute for fair dealings and quality products" (1990, page 23).

Additional Research Findings

Other components of the CCCU Resource Development Survey included public relations and development expenditures, and evaluation of the size of clerical and professional PR staffs. Public relations expenditures included salaries, benefits, travel, and media/promotion budgets. Basically, the larger Christian colleges spent more for public relations activities. Schools at the high and low ends of the enrollment scale spent less on PR activities in 1994 than in 1989, with institutions under 500 students decreasing their expenditures significantly. However, the overall survey mean rose by $12,151 or 9.1 percent.

Table 6-3
Public Relations Expenditures by Enrollment Size

Enrollment	1994 High	1989 High	1994 Low	1989 Low	1994 Mean	1989 Mean
Up to 500	$93,000	$209,666	$0	$29,638	$35,794	$73,513
501-750	399,577	152,589	46,664	10,000	134,996	64,584
751-1000	207,500	255,000	42,006	20,765	117,547	89,155
1001-1250	350,000	184,432	47,772	29,627	158,272	107,088
1251-1500	242,000	167,620	70,000	65,325	155,000	99,419
1501-2000	250,327	525,000	48,000	118,001	131,489	256,647
2001+	470,018	414,952	58,594	122,417	186,228	241,373
Survey Mean of All Groups					128,431	116,280

A similar trend developed with respect to percentage of total resource development expenditures. From 1989 to 1994, the largest and smallest of the CCCU schools reduced their expenditures on public relations activities. The result was a decline in the overall survey mean of 1.4 percent during the five years. The complete figures are presented in Table 6-4.

Table 6-4
Public Relations Expenditures: Percentage of Total Resource Development Expenditures by Enrollment Size

Enrollment	1994 High	1989 High	1994 Low	1989 Low	1994 Mean	1989 Mean
Up to 500	20.8	29.8	0.0	6.3	7.5	16.8
501-750	24.2	43.8	5.2	2.5	17.4	12.7
751-1000	21.3	30.2	5.1	4.3	14.7	14.0
1001-1250	29.3	26.7	9.7	3.8	15.9	12.4
1251-1500	34.1	12.7	7.1	10.5	17.8	11.8
1501-2000	17.3	39.6	2.6	8.4	11.7	20.5
2001+	22.9	25.5	3.3	7.0	10.2	20.1
Survey Mean of All Groups					13.7	15.1

The size of public relations staffs within Christian colleges is outlined in Tables 6-5 and 6-6. During the five-year period since the last survey, the larger schools made gains in number of professional staff members employed in public relations activities. The smallest schools reported declines since 1989. With respect to clerical staff members, the smallest schools again suffered losses. The largest schools held steady or increased slightly.

Table 6-5
Public Relations Professional Personnel (FTE) by Enrollment Size

Enrollment	1994 Mean	1989 Mean	1994 Mean	1989 Mean	1994 Mean	1989 Mean
Up to 500	2.00	2.50	.25	0.00	1.03	0.80
501-750	3.00	5.00	0.00	0.00	1.31	1.30
751-1000	4.30	4.00	1.00	0.00	1.95	1.50
1001-1250	3.25	4.50	1.00	0.80	2.00	2.20
1251-1500	3.00	2.80	.25	1.00	1.40	2.00
1501-2000	6.00	5.00	1.00	1.00	2.10	2.40
2001+	7.00	6.00	0.00	1.00	2.80	3.20
Survey Mean of All Groups					1.80	1.80

Table 6-6
Public Relations Clerical/Secretarial Staffing (FTE) by Enrollment Size

Enrollment	1994 Mean	1989 Mean	1994 Mean	1989 Mean	1994 Mean	1989 Mean
Up to 500	1.00	2.00	0.00	0.00	0.30	0.70
501-750	1.00	5.00	0.00	0.00	0.50	0.60
751-1000	3.00	2.00	0.00	0.00	0.80	0.80
1001-1250	2.00	2.00	0.00	0.00	0.90	0.90
1251-1500	1.00	1.00	0.50	1.00	0.80	0.60
1501-2000	3.00	3.00	0.00	0.00	1.10	1.30
2001+	4.00	2.00	0.00	0.00	1.00	1.00
Survey Mean of All Groups					0.75	0.80

Institutional Communications: the Ties that Bind

As public relations professionals, we are called upon daily to communicate with our constituencies. Kalman Druck identifies six key channels through which our communications efforts travel. They are: publications, publicity (the editorial use of mass media), advertising (the paid use of the mass media), audio-visuals, special events, and personal contact (1988, page 3). In the following paragraphs, we'll discuss these channels and one other current technological phenomenon: communicating on the Internet.

The Power of Publications

"Hey Jan, get a load of this."

Graphic designer Pete Font walked into his boss' office and dropped a lime-green brochure on her desk.

Jan Target, Hopeful College's PR director, picked up the paper and read the words, "Pastor's Newsletter."

"Where'd you get this?" queried Target as she thumbed through the panels.

"From my pastor," said Font. "Apparently the church relations people mailed them to all the ministers in our denomination."

Target continued to peruse the piece in silence. Clip art of various sizes and shapes was crammed between uneven columns of typewritten copy. Press-type headlines snaked above the faded paragraphs like jumbled Scrabble tiles. A silhouetted photo of the president, apparently cut out with dull scissors, smiled up at him beside the heading "Quality Counts at Hopeful College."

Picking up her phone, Target's fingers punched in the church relations number. "Hello, this is Jan Target in PR. May I speak to Tony please? Tell him it's about his pastor's newsletter..."

We all hope this scenario won't happen at our institution—at least not very often, because we understand that a publications program has a significant impact on shaping institutional image. Most people associate higher levels of education with quality. Therefore, incorporating quality points in all programs, and particularly in publications, can be a very positive addition to your institution's image. Marketing and public relations consultant Carol Halstead points to declining circulations and penetration of newspapers, magazines, and broadcast media as a bad sign for colleges, especially small colleges, that seek exposure in the mass media. (1993, page 122). Arden and Whalen in **Your Guide to Effective Publications** agree: "If an institution wants to prepare its own message, determine its format, and pick its audience, it cannot rely on the mass media. It must depend on printed publications to do this job" (1991, page 3).

Topor calls institutional publications "outreach materials." They include news releases, brochures, reports, flyers, newspaper ads, letters, viewbooks, catalogs, alumni magazines, invitations, newsletters, development case statements, etc. He suggests placing all these materials on a big table and conducting a publications audit by asking these questions: 1) what ideas are they selling? 2) what message does each deliver? 3) are the materials coordinated? 4) do they look like they came from the same place? 5) are they properly identified? 6) does the name of the institution appear on each? 7) does the copy suggest a common parent organization? and 8) does each institutional component represent itself separately at the expense of the parent institution? (1983, page 8).

Knowing why we produce publications in the first place is a critical component to any communications plan. "In public relations, there's a lot of discussion about 'behavioral PR,'" says John Soisson writing in **CASE Currents**, "...it helps PR pros shift their thinking to results, outcomes, the bottom line. So I suggest we start thinking about 'behavioral publications.' The term will help get us away from the design, the color, and the production schedule and move toward the real reason we do any publication (and the only reason we should): to influence behavior" (1994, page 14). This reminds us that publications aren't ends in themselves, but means to an end and should always be viewed and reviewed from that perspective.

Once the goals of a publications program have been established, some identifiable steps follow to insure operational success. Consider the following suggestions. First, gain control of the process. Second, coordinate your efforts. And, third, strive for consistency.

Control Comes from the Top

As Jan Target discovered in the preceding anecdote, gaining control over institutional publications can be difficult. Dan Forbush and Patricia Foster, writing in **CASE Currents**, describe the problem like this:

> Decentralized units—such as professional schools, medical centers, athletic departments, and schools of continuing education—routinely budget and staff their own PR operations. What's more, "corporate" operations dealing with key audiences—such as development, admissions, alumni, student and academic affairs—

often retain their own communications specialists as well. The
main problem that such "organized anarchy" poses for us is that
mixed messages undermine our efforts to position our institutions
and create positive public perceptions (1990, page 44).

This is not a problem limited to large universities. Even in small colleges the
element of control can be a problem if faculty and staff publish their own materials without professional guidance. The PR office (or some other designated office
staffed to handle these materials) should be both the policy setter and clearing-
house for institutional publications. Most always this will require an endorsement
from the highest levels of administration. But it's the only way to gain any form of
control over the messages being sent to off-campus constituencies.

Without this control, the institution risks: 1) fragmented, sometimes er-
ror-filled messages, 2) multiple designs, 3) wide swings in quality from piece to
piece, 4) loss of cost savings due to lack of expertise, and 5) duplication of programs and content. However, with the PR office screening the publications, there
are real benefits: 1) economies of resources, 2) coordination of institutional message, 3) coordination of design, 4) consistent reporting of accurate information,
and 5) assurance of overall quality.

Improve Your Coordination
Armed with the charge to produce quality publications, you can now turn your
attention to the everyday, nitty gritty of how to get it done. Simply put, the goals
of your program should revolve around four obvious, but sometimes elusive, elements: lucid writing; clean, organized design; professional photography, and efficient production.

With these elements in mind, here are some suggestions that can help you get a
handle on the publications you're asked to coordinate. You may be tempted to skip
a step from project to project; however, the consistent application of these principles (and others you've learned on your own) will bring the rewards you seek for
your program.

1. **Begin with planning.** Become proactive so that you control the publica-
    tions schedule, not the other way around. Develop a master publications
    schedule during early summer. Ask departments what publications they
    plan to publish and then compile a master list. Then send each department
    deadlines for copy preparation, design, printing, and delivery for their
    projects. Assign someone from your shop to each "client" to ensure all
    deadlines are met and the piece is delivered on time. Naturally, there are
    clients who, during the year, request projects not on the master list. How-
    ever, by planning the bulk of the projects in advance, the process is given
    structure and becomes significantly more manageable.

2. **Agree on the purpose of the publication.** Ask the purpose of the piece.
    What is it trying to accomplish? An even more basic question is "Do you
    really need a brochure, newsletter, etc.?" Occasionally a client wants a
    brochure for the wrong reasons: they like the one a colleague has, they've

got money in the budget which they'll lose if it isn't spent, etc. You may even be able to suggest an alternate form of communication that would better suit their needs.

3. **Focus on the audience.** Who does your client want to reach with this publication? James Grunig gives insightful information on audience analysis when he says: "You in campus communication must realize that your audience is not a vague mass but rather a set of specific, small audiences, each with distinct interests, concerns and attitudes. Your communication strategies, in turn, must vary for each subgroup according to its character" (1990, page 38).

4. **Identify the budget.** Determine the budget at your initial meeting. Experience will tell you if the budget matches the client's expectations or not. Then, when the project is underway, let the client know immediately of additional costs incurred. Better yet, let the client make the decision on whether or not to spend any additional money. It's his/her budget. Not informing the client of additional charges can make things awkward when the bill arrives.

5. **Commit to reasonable deadlines.** We all want to please our campus clients. But don't commit to delivery schedules that overtax your staff and resources (unless it's the boss that asks). Overall, however, be realistic and give yourself enough time.

6. **Keep the client informed.** This not only goes for financial items, but also for design. Show clients thumbnail sketches, drafts of copy, bluelines, etc.—whatever it takes for them to know what's going on. This process, although seemingly cumbersome at times, will alleviate any misgivings on the client's part about the finished product. In the publications business, nobody likes surprises.

7. **Establish written records.** Keep records on all jobs. Record each job in a log book. Then make a job folder that contains a specification sheet with all data pertinent to the completion of the piece (e.g. client name, budget number, typesetting and printing specs, billable time, deadlines, etc.). It's amazing how valuable these folders are the next year the same job needs to be reprinted.

8. **File artwork and printed samples.** There's nothing more frustrating than getting an order to reprint a piece and not being able to locate the artwork. Having a logical, complete artwork file (along with printed samples) will save you time and money in the future.

9. **Create a freelance pool of writers and designers.** If your office is like ours, we get more requests to coordinate projects than we can handle. To solve this problem, we've identified a cadre of freelance designers and writers who are an extension of our office. Through instruction and expe-

rience over time, they know what we need and deliver it accordingly. This concept will significantly expand your ability to serve campus needs.

10. **Develop a photo file.** This certainly is not a novel idea. However, it's a significant one. Equally, or perhaps even more important, is the quality of photos you put in your file. Don't shave dollars when it comes to quality photography. Work with a professional. Budget creatively (e.g. pull several client budgets together to hire a freelancer for a day, etc.). Whatever it takes, strive for good, and current, photography.

11. **Just say no!** When clients present rush jobs that are truly unreasonable, don't be afraid to say you just can't handle it (assuming you can't). Instead, shift the burden back onto them by offering a name from your freelance pool for them to contact. However, insist on seeing the appropriate proofs from the freelancer before the job is printed.

Strive for Consistency
Achieving control and coordination over time leads to consistency. Consistency is important for several reasons. First, consistency in message and design reinforces your institutional image. Halstead says key messages and themes should be repeated over and over in a public relations program to create and reinforce the institution's image (1993, page 117). Second, consistency creates confidence, which is critical to building trust on and off campus. Obtaining the confidence of those in authority will allow you to receive the encouragement and resource support you need to continue a quality publications program. In the process, don't forget to market your expertise. If you're producing quality materials, everyone will be proud. Announce any awards in the faculty/staff newsletter and deliver samples of all completed pieces to upper administration regularly. Third, consistency avoids confusion. "Too many institutions change logos, colors and key messages in response to the desires of a new president or just because they are tired of them. A lesson from the advertising business would apply: It takes years to establish an image, and changing it frequently confuses the audience" (1993, page 122).

Designing on the Desktop
No discussion about publications would be complete without mentioning desktop publishing (DTP). Just as the word processor has revolutionized the way we write, so the advent of DTP systems has redefined the publications process.

Perhaps most important to remember is that a desktop system, no matter how sophisticated the software and equipment, does not replace the need for a qualified graphic designer. Once I met with a visitor from another college who was planning to purchase hardware and software for desktop publishing. When asked how he was going to fund the system, he replied he was planning to use the salary line for his current designer because DTP, he thought, would eliminate that position. This would have been a mistake because a good designer is the key to DTP, not the other way around.

Desktop systems are tools to help a good designer do a better job. And the design of your publications is best left to them. However, if you aren't a designer and still wish to use DTP in your office, there are many software programs and training courses available. At minimum, you'll want a professional to critique your efforts to insure the overall quality and continuity of your publications program.

One word of caution. Because of the proliferation of easy-to-obtain and use desktop graphics, many of your colleagues around campus will dive into designing their own pieces. Some of these "home-made" efforts can be frightening. The answer again lies in the control issue, that is, obtaining a policy endorsed by top administration that routes all would-be publications through the public relations office prior to production. Your proactive work in explaining your services around campus, coupled with the consistency factor discussed above, will make this process more streamlined and effective.

Publicity and the Mass Media

"This is Jan Target," said Hopeful College's PR director, picking up her phone.

"Hello, Jan, Jim Brown in religion calling. I need your help. Our department is sponsoring a symposium in two weeks that's probably the biggest thing we've done in years."

"Oh?" responded Target, fumbling for a pencil and yellow notepad, "tell me about it."

"Well, the symposium topic is 'Jonah and the Dead Sea Scrolls.' Our keynote speaker is Jason Salt from Waterville College in New York. Let me tell you, he's a BIG name on this subject."

"I see," said Target, scribbling cryptic notes.

"We need publicity and fast," said Brown. "We need advance notice in the newspapers so we can build a crowd. I've talked to Dr. Salt and he's set aside time for a press conference. And I really think some ads in the local papers would be good, but we're really tight on budget. Can you help?"

"Uh, you've kind of caught me by surprise," Target said, her pencil lead breaking on the yellow pad. "I'll see what I can do."

One of the major tasks of the public relations office is publicizing campus programs, people, and activities. Publicity involves placing stories in the mass media (radio, newspapers, magazines, or television). "Placing" in this case refers to either: a) creation of the message by the institution (e.g. news release, PSA, etc.) and given to the media or b) creation by others (e.g. a feature story by a reporter). The first example is controlled by the institution (assuming the story is reproduced verbatim) and the second is controlled by the media. (One might argue that all stories are controlled by the media, but that's another story.)

As Professor Brown in our previous anecdote illustrates, many campus clients have unrealistic expectations of what publicity and the PR office can accomplish. Here are three examples:

1. **Press releases will automatically produce an audience.** Press releases are best used to create awareness and convey pertinent information for an idea or event (Hollister, 1990, page 33). To ensure people will act on the information, other tactics should be used to reinforce the original message

(e.g. personal contact by the institution, personal contact by peers, targeted letters, etc.). A PR strategy that includes a mix of these tactics has a much better chance of delivering the desired results.

2. **Everyone will share the client's enthusiasm for the program.** You may have to diplomatically explain to your Professor Brown that although his program is certainly interesting, his best chance of success is seeking to reach others who have similar interests in this area. As Rayburn and Preston remind us, "We can't rely anymore on the mass media to deliver a message to our audience. In fact, the mass audience has all but ceased to exist. In its place are fragmented subaudiences that respond to the media selectively, if at all" (1990, page 28). These subaudiences have distinct interests, concerns, and attitudes. Whatever communication strategies are employed must vary according to the character of the subaudience (Grunig, 1990, page 38).

3. **Lead time, what's that?** First of all, the Professor Browns who call will often not understand that you have other projects that have been well planned in advance. Second, clients often don't realize that a coordinated strategy for these types of requests takes time to plan and implement. And third, don't forget reporters need lead time, too. Don't expect immediate response when you call. Find out deadlines and plan ahead. The goal is to satisfy both parties in a timely way.

Promoting your institution or program through publicity is both an art and a science. The art comes in recognizing a good story and telling it in such a way that it reaches the target audience and delivers the desired information. The science of publicity involves the tools of the trade and their appropriate use.

The baseline element of publicity that affects all the other tools is media relations. Developing good relationships with reporters, assignment editors is imperative, but, as you have probably already learned, your agenda and the media's are not often the same.

> The media frequently focus on the least significant but more colorful phases of academe. It is hardly news that a certain class met at its regularly scheduled time and discussed the material set forth in the syllabus. And yet this is what higher education is really about and not the homecoming parades, athletic contests and student demonstrations. To make something newsworthy out of the mundane occurrences is the real challenge (Reilly, 1981, page 423).

Elements of Good Media Relations
Although a working knowledge of media relations can come only from experience, here are some beneficial guidelines to follow:

1. **Find your niche.** Ask "What are my institution's strengths?" "Which faculty members are doing things of interest to the public?" One advancement professional put it this way: "Our true strength comes from faculty and students and administrators on the inside. We need to get out of our offices and interact with internal constituents—to attend lectures and to talk about issues that concern them" (Moore, 1988, page 18). This process will increase your campus credibility and identify marketable stories and features for the media.

2. **Develop relationships with reporters.** It's very important that you introduce yourself to reporters assigned to cover higher education in your area. Familiarize them with your institution. Ask what type of stories they prefer. For example, at SPU, we took the higher education writers at our two major dailies to lunch. We discovered one reporter preferred more human interest material and warm feature stories. The other, by contrast, only wanted issue-oriented items. These two lunches have given us valuable insight into which stories to place with whom.

3. **Use press releases sparingly.** There's still a place for the press release (whether electronic or conventional). However, it should not substitute for personal contact with reporters and targeted strategies for publicizing a particular person or program.

4. **Treat reporters equally.** Whenever possible, don't play favorites with reporters. You will share different levels of information with a weekly paper as opposed to a major daily. However, be sensitive not to appear biased one over another so that you will be perceived as fair, reflecting favorably on your program and giving you more future credibility.

5. **Be responsive to media inquiries.** Answer media inquiries courteously and quickly. If you don't know the answer to questions, say so. Then research the answer and get back to them. If the answer involves bad news, confer with your administrator and then deliver the information candidly. Stonewalling or stalling is the worst possible strategy. Openness and honesty contribute to a credible, long-term relationship with your institution and the media.

6. **Target the source.** Match the message to the medium. If your story is visual, consider TV; if more verbal than visual, look to radio. Also be sure to send business articles to the business writer, science stories to the science writer.

7. **Don't peddle weak stories.** Just as you are selective on when to use a news release, so you should also screen the newsworthiness of stories you promote to reporters.

8. **Prioritize your outlets.** An ongoing question in Christian higher education concerns publicity efforts directed toward the secular media vs.

church constituencies. The answer depends on the college's priorities. Ideally, both would be pursued. However, some institutions find it difficult to get attention from major dailies, because they exist in a large and competitive media market. Such institutions may have more success through church channels. Other schools in smaller media markets may be quite successful in promoting their programs through the secular media, which in turn reaches church constituencies as well. Each school should seek its own balance.

9. **Make use of technology: the Internet explosion.** Technology is creating unprecedented opportunities for new forms of communication, some of which directly affect media relations. The Internet, the information "superhighway," allows anyone with access to a computer and a modem the ability to tap into databases around the world. The increased use and popularity of the Internet has spawned a variety of services now available to public relations professionals. ProfNet, for example, an electronic cooperative that links reporters with campus news and public relations officers, receives reporter queries through e-mail, fax, or phone and forwards them to its members in two daily digests via the Internet. Notes Patricia Faccipointi in **CASE Currents**, "Public information officers respond with targeted facts, pithy quotes and contact numbers" (1995, page 24). Currently 800 schools subscribe to the service. A similar service can be found on CompuServe's "Journalism Forum," where reporters offer their needs and campus news officers pitch stories to match them. Other campuses send news releases directly into newsrooms via e-mail. Still others create online "home pages" where reporters can tap into printed news releases, faculty resources, or even letters from the president.

On the plus side, all colleges can benefit from this new technology. As Forbush and Toon note in **CASE Currents**, "Reporters will use technology to cast a wider net for sources. With computer networks, your campus is accessible to the media no matter what its size or location" (1994, page 46). However, the flip side is that having a home page probably won't garner any national media coverage you couldn't get in other ways, says Bob Fisher in **CASE Currents,** but it is a new tool that provides an easy, inexpensive way to offer text and graphics to almost anyone (1995, page 33).

The Role of Advertising

Advertising offers your institution one distinct advantage over publicity: you can control the message and the medium. As opposed to publicity, which is free, advertising involves paying a fee to secure space or time to present a particular message. Where publicity and public relations are management functions, advertising is a marketing function because it relates to the selling of goods and services (Reilly, 1981, page 5).

Advertising is a popular means of soliciting prospective students within Christian higher education as evidenced by the number of college-guide magazines and recruitment card decks currently available. This fact makes advertising decisions even more significant.

Like it or not, if you are advertising in a Christian publication, you are competing for attention with every other college and university within its pages. And that space isn't cheap. Therefore, it's to your advantage to maximize your money and your message in your campaign. Engleberg and Topor, writing in **CASE Currents**, advise that "while creating your ad campaign, ask yourself this crucial question and keep asking it: To whom are we directing this ad? Don't plan ads for internal audiences when you really intend to appeal to external targets, and don't try to be everything to everybody" (1994, page 15). This advice is especially important for smaller institutions with limited budgets. Good advertising doesn't have to be full-page and four-color to work. But it does have to be well-planned for maximum cost-effectiveness and results.

With that starting point in mind, here are some suggestions on how to proceed with an advertising campaign:

1. **Define your objectives**. Before you even talk about design, sit down and create a communications plan that includes message, medium, audience, and what you want to accomplish.

2. **Identify your institutional distinctives**. Determine what significant characteristics set your school apart from others. Build your design and message around them.

3. **Seek professional help**. This may merely mean walking down the hall to your designer's office, or, if you don't have a staff designer, it may mean seeking an advertising agency, design firm, or faculty person from your art department. Creating the ad(s) for your campaiagn should be placed in the capable hands of professionals.

4. **Monitor your results**. Keep track of responses. Tracking them over time will allow you to accurately evaluate both ad content and media placement for future campaigns.

Other Channels of Communications

The last three of Druck's channels of communication include audio-visuals, special events and personal contact. As mentioned earlier, another channel that has burst onto the communications landscape is the Internet. Although its widespread impact was unforeseen just a few years ago, the "Net" is revolutionizing the way we communicate to target audiences. A brief discussion of each of these channels of communication identifies their role in the overall public relations plan.

Getting Up to Speed on the "I-way"

The information superhighway, as it's called, is offering communications connections in an unprecedented fashion. Robert Duffy and Michael Palmer write, "This network already links more than 15 million users at universities and companies world wide, and it is expanding at a rate approaching five percent a month" (1994, page 26). Faccipointi concurs in **CASE Currents**: "Electronic communication is quickly becoming the method of choice for many of the people you most want to reach. Millions of progressive journalists, sharp students, and savvy alumni have access to the Internet. The rest are trying to figure out how to get there—and how to deal with it when they do" (1995, page 22).

A new set of terms has or will soon become a familiar operative for campus public relations officers: "Mosaic," "Netscape," "World Wide Web," "Universal Resource Locators (URL)," "Web Server." One of these terms needs further discussion: World Wide Web (WWW). The WWW is a subset of the Internet that displays information using a combination of text, sound and motion graphics. Through "browser" software programs like Mosaic and Netscape, you can visit a multitude of Web sites, including a growing number of colleges and universities through their "home pages." These home pages, or visual addresses, allow an electronic entrance to campuses across the country. "Browsers" may then view and interact with graphics and information about the school.

"The Web...opens up new ways for us to reach prospective students, keep in touch with alumni and provide information to the media," says Fisher writing in **CASE Currents**. "We can show off our specialties to interested citizens, potential students and opinion leaders" (1995, page 33). Fisher believes the key audience for electronic targeting may be prospective students because of the increase in schools, from elementary to high school, that are plugging into the Internet. That means viewbooks, catalogs, campus tours, financial aid documents, and a host of other recruiting items become candidates for electronic transfer. Says Fisher, "Creating a presence on the Web allows you to represent the strengths and spirit of your campus to an audience that is overwhelmingly young, computer-sophisticated and curious" (1995, page 33). Of course, establishing this presence on the Web doesn't happen by accident. It takes a combined effort of public relations and computer information systems personnel to achieve the final product. But the results can be exciting.

Your Campus on Video and CD-ROM

The promotional video has been a popular recruitment tool in recent years. As more and more institutions began using video, the same challenge that confronts recruitment publications came into play: how to create something that stands out from the crowd.

A campus video is not unique anymore, and it remains a high-ticket item to produce. However, it still can be a powerful weapon in the recruitment arsenal, especially if used in creative new ways. One new application is the use of video on "home pages" (see above for discussion). Uses of video other than admissions recruiting include fundraising, alumni relations, and faculty recruiting. Media relations may send TV stations video clips of campus experts. Your video may also run on cable TV for viewing by local communities. Still other schools have extended the traditional boundaries by giving videos the jobs publications used to do (e.g. video annual reports that run as TV PSAs) (Wright, 1989, page 20).

Because of relatively expensive professional production costs, the key to successful campus videos is to use footage in as many applications as possible. Careful planning at the front end of the project can produce significant results.

Some schools have taken the step into multimedia and CD-ROM technology to promote their campuses and programs. Multimedia applications include computer-mediated communication that integrates any of these elements: text, audio, graphics, photo stills, animation, and video. As Duffy and Palmer note, "CD-ROM technology is the magic bullet for handling multimedia, which takes up lots of space. A single disk can hold the text of nearly a thousand conventional books and about 40 minutes of full-screen video with soundtrack" (1994, page 26). With multimedia-equipped PCs outselling all others, the audience for this powerful form of communication will continue to grow exponentially.

Making Your Events Special

A form of communication that all colleges use in one shape or another is the special event. Examples include alumni banquets, inaugurations, fundraising dinners, commencements, special speakers, musical events, auctions, and academic forums, to name a few. Not many things we do consume as much concentrated staff time, energy, and resources as creating, developing, and coordinating a special event. That's why it's crucial that each event be critically analyzed before you plunge into it.

"Perhaps the most important aspect of designing any affair is to determine its objectives," say Tom Martin and Linda Adams, special events consultants (1989, page 20). They advocate asking the same questions you would ask when planning a publications or advertising campaign. For example: 1) what is the purpose of the event? 2) who is the audience? 3) does the audience have any expectations? 4) what do you want the event to accomplish? 5) what amount of staff time can be committed to the event? and 6) what is the budget?

Remember that at the heart of all memorable events is creativity—in theme, promotions, staging, and program. By combining these elements with clear objectives, you can go into the process with a plan and come out with your sanity and a successful event.

Personal Contact

Despite the efficiencies and opportunities that new technology offers in public relations, finding a way to make the message personal remains the most important factor in achieving communication success. Halstead affirms that the higher the degree of personalization in a message, the more effective the message will likely be. Below are the most commonly used means of communication, listed in order of their effectiveness:

1. One-to-one, face-to-face conversation

2. Small group discussions or meetings of five people or fewer

3. Speaking before a group where questions and dialogue are encouraged

4. Telephone conversation between two people

5. Handwritten, personal letter

6. Typewritten personal letter that clearly was not generated from a computer database or typed by an automatic machine

7. Computer-generated or word-processed "personal letter"

8. Mass-produced, nonpersonal letter

9. Brochure or pamphlet sent out as a "direct mail" piece without a cover letter

10. Newsletters, magazines, tabloids developed and distributed by the institution

11. News carried in newspapers, radio, television, magazines

12. Advertising in newspapers, radio, television, magazines

13. Other forms of communication (billboards, skywriters) (1993, page 120).

The challenge is to incorporate the highest level of personalization into all of our marketing and public relations communications. For example, following up a news release with a personal phone call (or visit) maximizes your chances of successful communication.

Sometimes, a mass-media approach should be set aside for a more personalized strategy. Once a music administrator wanted to place ads in a national magazine for the purpose of obtaining prospects for his program. After some discussion, we agreed that a better plan would be to invest the money he had for the campaign into hiring a person to visit local high schools and talk to band and orchestra directors and music teachers and solicit referrals from them. The result was a significant increase in names of prospective music students and ultimately a better use of his promotional funds.

Looking Back to the Future

Rayburn and Preston state that our public relations activities should influence people's behavior—whether that behavior is giving to the annual fund, enrolling in our institutions or getting results from government officials (1990, page 29). As Christian advancement professionals, we must add God-honoring values and distinctives to that formula. Only then have we adequately defined the role of public relations in Christian higher education.

If Hopeful College's Jan Target would apply the foregoing principles of public relations, she needn't fear future appointments with her president. In fact, if President Goal were to visit the PR office, he'd likely see the following summary of Target's new approach to public relations posted on her wall:

1. Plan and plan again. You need a roadmap to reach your destination.

2. Conduct research. Discover your strengths and let them guide your efforts.

3. Project a consistent image. Seek an image of quality, but be sure it matches the reality of your programs.

4. Keep the channels of communication open. Whichever channel of communications you use, whether it's publications, publicity, advertising, special events, electronic multimedia or personal contact, use the right channel for the right job and strive for quality of presentation.

5. Remember the three C's. Control, coordination and consistency lead to efficient project management.

6. Measure and evaluate. Look back before you look ahead.

Finally, Jan Target would aim to make the bottom line her top priority, but only in the context of a biblically-based, values approach to public relations activities. Larry Johnston describes the idea by saying that to honor God and be effective in the contemporary marketplace, Christian marketers (e.g. public relations professionals) must strive for an optimum fit between God's value system and what constituents want (i.e. market demand) (1989, page 242). The outcome of this process provides the impetus for an effective public relations plan. Even more important, it rewards us with the knowledge that we're advancing the kingdom of God through Christian higher education.

RESOURCES

Burkett, Larry. **Business by the Book**. Nashville: Thomas Nelson Publishers, 1990.

Bonnet, Susan. "Taking the Broad View. Use Your Institution's Strategic Plan as a Road Map for PR." **CASE Answer File: Developing a PR Plan**. CASE: 1988.

Dayton, Edward R. and Engstrom, Ted W. **Strategy for Leadership**. New Jersey: Fleming H. Revell Co., 1979.

Druck, Kalman B. "Advancement Planning. An Objective View: Keep Your Eye on Your Goals." **CASE Answer File: Developing A PR Plan**. CASE: 1988.

Duffy, Robert A., and Palmer, Michael J. "How Multimedia Technologies Will Influence PR Practice." **Public Relations Quarterly**, Spring 1994.

Engleberg, Moshe and Topor, Robert. "The Advertising Advantage." **CASE Currents**, September 1994.

Faccipointi, Patricia A. "Network News." **CASE Currents**, January 1995.

Fisher, Bob. "The Web We Weave." **CASE Currents**, January 1995.

Forbush, Dan and Foster, Patricia A. "Building Coherent Communications." **CASE Currents**, March 1990.

Forbush, Dan and Toon, John. "PR in the 21st Century." **CASE Currents**, March 1994.

Grunig, James E. "Focus on Your Audience." **CASE Currents**, February 1990.

Halstead, Carol P. "Effective Public Relations and Communications Strategies." **Winning Strategies in Challenging Times for Advancing Small Colleges**. Ed. by Wesley K. Willmer. Washington, DC: Council for the Advancement and Support of Education (CASE), 1993.

Harrison, Thomas. Public Relations session at the Christian Management Institute, Anaheim, California, February 1990.

Hollister, Peter H. "Putting Theory to Work." **CASE Currents**, February 1990.

Johnston, Larry. "Strategic Planning: Spirit Driven or Market Driven?" **Money for Ministries**. Ed. by Wesley K. Willmer. Wheaton, Illinois: Victor Books, 1989.

Marken, G.A. "Andy." "Corporate Image: We All Have One, But Few Work to Protect and Project It." **Public Relations Quarterly**, Spring 1990.

Martin, Tom and Adams, Linda. "Planning Programs with Punch." **CASE Currents**, November/December 1989.

Moore, Keith. "Position Your PR Office." **CASE Currents**, March 1989.

Moriarty, Sandra E. "PR and IMC: The Benefits of Integration." **Public Relations Quarterly**, Fall 1994.

Rayburn, J.D. II and Preston, Thomas L. "The Science Behind Public Relations." **CASE Currents**, February 1990.

Reilly, Robert T. **Public Relations in Action**. New Jersey: Prentice-Hall, Inc., 1981.

Sevier, Robert A. "Why Marketing Plans Fail." **CASE Currents**, November/December 1994.

Soisson, John. "Mind Your Business." **CASE Currents**, March 1994.

Topor, Robert. **Marketing Higher Education, A Practical Guide.** Washington DC: Council for the Advancement and Support of Education (CASE), 1983.

Webster, Phillip J., APR. "What's the Bottom Line?" **Public Relations Journal**, February 1990.

Willmer, Wesley K. **Funds, Friends and Freshmen for Christian Colleges**. Washington DC: Christian College Coalition, 1987.

Wright, William R. "For Your Eyes Only." **CASE Currents**, March 1989.

About the Author

JOHN L. GLANCY is director of university relations at Seattle Pacific University, Seattle, Washington. He earned a bachelor's degree in English and business at Seattle Pacific in 1970 and a master's degree in communications from the University of Washington in 1979. Professionally, he is active in CASE, most recently serving as communications track chair for the CASE District VIII annual conference. John resides in Redmond, Washington, with his wife, Sally, and their children, Nick, 15, and Angie, 7. A recreational runner, biker, and swimmer, he also enjoys watching and coaching youth sports—especially when his kids are on the field, pitch, or court.

Chapter 7

Trustees: Their Essential Leadership Function

ROBERT C. ANDRINGA

Good Christian college and university advancement begins with the board of trustees. As stewards of the institution, Christian college board members are ultimately responsible to God for the direction their institution takes by upholding its mission and establishing its vision for the future. According to Robert Gale, former long-time president of the Association of Governing Boards of Universities and Colleges (AGB), the boards role in advancement is critical. Gale states, "Without help from the governing board, institutions cannot be expected to reach fund raising goals they set for themselves" (1989, page 102).

The board's role in advancement goes well beyond that of raising funds. Their involvement in public relations, admissions, and alumni relations are equally critical to the institution's health and welfare. R. Judson Carlberg, president of Gordon College and a former chief development officer, put it this way: "The fund development efforts of small colleges require strong trusteeship. Good trustees not only are committed to generating resources, they also insist on good governance practices which strengthen an institution's mission. The result? An effective advancement program!"

This chapter is designed to assist the 2,800 or more trustees of Christian colleges and universities and their executives advance their institutions and meet this unique challenge of trusteeship. While there are plenty of "how to" books and manuals on trusteeship in general, this chapter attempts to address the institutional advancement concerns for Christian college board members without duplicating existing literature. This chapter outlines 10 key functions of the board that relate to an advancement-conscientious board member. They are:

1. Clarify the mission for effective advancement

2. Assume an advancement-sensitive strategic plan and goals

3. Establish policies to guide advancement efforts

4. Select and nurture an advancement-skilled president

5. Ensure financial solvency and integrity

6. Recruit and train advancement-oriented trustees

7. Learn the board's governance model

8. Participate in advancement work

9. Promote advancement committee effectiveness

10. Evaluate for maximum advancement effectiveness

Board members fulfill these functions in the context of wearing one or more of three hats—those of governance, volunteer, or implementor. It is imperative that all board members understand and function within these distinctions.

1. **Governance Hat.** Worn only when a meeting is properly called and a quorum is present, this hat is worn relatively few hours in a year, and it is always worn in a group decision-making setting. Once out of a meeting, no trustee has authority to set policy for the institution and must remove this hat.

2. **Volunteer Hat.** This second hat is worn most often. Between board meetings, when a trustee is having lunch with the president, offering advice via phone or fax, visiting an alumni group, or asking a colleague to support the institution, a trustee is functioning in a volunteer capacity. A trustee has no more "clout" than anyone else in those situations and must be careful not to assume the governance hat authority.

3. **Implementor Hat.** Once in a while, a board will grant to an individual or small group of trustees the authority to implement board policy. Normally board policy is implemented by the president, but there are exceptions. An example might be a board that grants authority to a finance committee to chose a contractor or an investment management firm.

As you read this chapter, you will find reference to trustee-related data taken from a 1994 survey sponsored by the Coalition for Christian Colleges & Universities (CCCU) with funding from the Lilly Endowment, Inc. This survey was distributed to Coalition member institutions with the purpose of exploring trends related to institutional advancement at Christian colleges and universities, including the role of the board of trustees.

Before getting into the specific advancement functions of trusteeship, consider first the profile of the typical Coalition board. The survey found that on average:

- There are 30 voting members on the board
- 13 percent are female
- 4 percent are persons of color
- 10 percent feel adequately trained in fundraising

- 71 percent are required to be in a particular denomination
- 52 percent are appointed by a denomination
- 39 percent are alumni of the college

In addition, the occupational distribution of trustees follows these patterns:

- 25 percent are clergy
- 45 percent are in business
- 12 percent are in the field of education
- 5 percent are lawyers
- 5 percent are medical doctors

Function 1: Clarify the mission for effective advancement.

A central function of the board is to assure clarity of mission. Richard Chait states that "mission definition is not a task that is done once and then forgotten. It requires constant monitoring and regular restatement or reaffirmation by the board" (July 1988, page 19). Connie Growther, in an article titled, "Building a Better Board," adds that "knowing the [institution's] mission is the first step toward effective advancement" (November 1989, page 22f).

The board is the keeper of the vision and mission for a Christian college or university. It is not enough to adopt some well-sounding prose for the catalog. Boards must work hard to clarify distinctives, values, and outcomes of attendance at their institutions compared to others. A clear mission statement should guide all elements of the campus in day-to-day decision-making. Wally Hobbs suggests this applies particularly to the advancement office. "Unless the institution advancement officer is able to convey the college's vision, purpose, and character to others in terms they can understand, advancement is an empty exercise, for there is really nothing to advance (1981, page 21).

One of our campuses, Trinity Western University, tests each program—even each class—as to how well it contributes to the accomplishment of this mission:

> The mission of Trinity Western University as an arm of the Church is to develop godly Christian leaders: positive, goal-oriented university graduates with thoroughly Christian minds; growing disciples of Jesus Christ who glorify God through fulfilling The Great Commission, serving God and man in the various marketplaces of life.

This and most mission statements are adopted after months of good dialogue among faculty, administrators, staff, and students, as well as trustees. Without the board insisting on such a process, this critical step in institutional excellence is often neglected.

But it is not enough just to adopt a statement like that of Trinity Western. The board must constantly ask for information that assures that the mission and other statements of values are, in fact, the driving force behind policies and practice. As Hurtubise and Bishop say, "Ownership of the institution's mission that is shared by the president and the board provides the foundation for solid advancement efforts (March 1991, page 33).

Function 2: Assure an advancement-sensitive strategic plan and goals.

An important function is to approve the major goals of the institution which then influence the priorities for the advancement efforts. At the broadest level, those goals should clarify answers to the questions: "Which benefits, for whom, at what cost (priorities)?"

Few boards engage in writing strategic plans, but they should insist that a good campus-wide planning process is on-going. Some boards approve a "board-level" strategic plan, then charge the president with developing a planning process that results in other clear goals and objectives for all units of the campus.

Part of a long-range plan should be goals that relate to advancement: enrollment targets, criteria for admission, the major academic programs to be offered, relationship to the community, capital campaigns, and unrestricted giving goals. None of these decisions come easy and the trustees must be wise in their approval of goals which may cause controversy on campus.

Wayne Clugston states, "Unless there is leadership, institutional goals will not be established or clearly stated. Without such goals, the institutional advancement officer has nothing to advance" (1981, page 6). The board must assure that advancement-aware goals are in place.

Function 3: Establish policies to guide advancement efforts.

The board should establish policies that empower the president and staff to fulfill their marketing, public relations, and fundraising goals. These policies must reflect the Christian standards for which our institutions should be known. The pressures to meet deadlines and monetary goals are immense at times. Sound policy, monitored and adjusted as necessary, contributes to success and eases the burden on senior executives.

At the broadest level, the board must be clear on "which benefits, for whom, at what cost." These are not easy "ends" issues to resolve. Left unclear, the institution will either drift or be pulled apart by different units heading in their own directions. Boards must focus on the results the institution seeks and then provide positive, realistic parameters within which administrators and faculty can provide leadership to achieve the desired ends.

Ideally, all standing policies of the board should be contained in one document. Otherwise, boards lose track of previous policies hidden in board minutes which seldom get reviewed over time. These policies should provide the parameters within which the president is allowed to run the institution.

Dr. John Carver, who popularized the "policy governance model," challenges boards to keep all on-going policies on less than 15 pages! He and others argue that most boards get drawn far more into the various "means" of an institution rather than focusing on results and giving the administrators some parameters within which they can exercise their professional judgments.

Function 4: Select an advancement-skilled president.

John W. Nason, one of the leading authorities on academic and foundation governance, says, "The president is the central and most important individual in the governance of any college or university. His or her selection is, therefore, of paramount importance to the well-being of the institution" (1989). This holds true for the advancement function as well. In the last two decades, the president's role has become decisively more advancement-related. In a study of Christian colleges (see Dowden chapter), presidents indicated that they spend 44 percent of their time in advancement-related activities (1990, page 24).

For the Christ-centered college, the challenge of selecting one person to satisfy so many constituencies and expectations is critical, but almost every stakeholder wants an advancement-oriented president who can represent the institution outside the campus as well as lead internally. For a new president to do this well, a board should already have achieved high marks on the first three functions listed above. How trustees should conduct presidential searches, involving faculty, administrators, alumni and other stakeholders is a book in itself (see Neff in the resource list at the end).

Once selected, the on-going relationship between the president and board is critical. The chairperson must manage the board, and the board must let the president lead. Still, the board, through its standing policies and its required reports, must provide for reasonable accountability without getting itself into management.

Whether they realize it or not, trustees send many signals to people on the campus which get translated into affirmation or perceived criticism. People are the most important asset of any college, and the board, through good policies and non-governance acts of good will, can do much to create a healthy environment.

Here is where the love and caring of mature Christian trustees can make a huge difference in the campus culture. Biblical principles abound on how to build relationships, and trustees can model a high level of obedience to them.

Function 5: Ensure financial solvency and integrity.

The board cannot delegate to the president or anyone else ultimate responsibility for the financial stability and integrity of the institution. This requires good board policies not only to guide fundraising activities, but tuition, operating expenditures, capital projects, investments, etc.—no small task for complicated institutions with a sizable physical plant and many people!

It is difficult to be optimistic about the financial futures of our institutions. A respected economist and former small college president, David Breneman summarized his research of several colleges this way: "Colleges are pursuing several organizational and strategic changes designed to lower the rate of cost escalation, thereby helping to hold down the rate of future tuition increases. The search for increased revenue is focused mainly on development efforts" (1994, page 101).

Breneman's conclusion that fundraising is the key is obvious to careful observers who know that federal and state student aid is unlikely to keep up with inflation, that people are already resisting current sticker prices, and that our institutions have very little endowment to hold them steady through difficult years. The current trends of discounting tuition, deferring maintenance, holding faculty salaries behind those in other institutions when the market is becoming highly competitive for good academics, drawing down endowments—these are only some of the critical issues facing trustees today.

Beyond questions of solvency, however, are other critical roles in finance. Integrity in how funds are raised and spent, invested, and accounted for must be of concern to trustees who know the moral character of their institution is part of being a steward of the assets to which God has entrusted them.

Function 6: Recruit and train advancement-oriented trustees.

New trustees should be recruited according to a "board profile" developed in advance which identifies the kind of experience, talent, and motivation the board needs to fill all its functions. Think of putting together a professional football team. Owners and coaches know they need more than just good athletes who know the rules of football. They need players to fill each of 11 positions on both offense and defense, plus special teams players, so they keep their scouts working constantly to identify, by name and other relevant data, players who can fill specific roles.

Boards need to think more this way. What kind of expertise and skills do we need? What would make for a balanced team (board)? Good boards write out selection criteria they want *all* potential trustees to meet, e.g., mature Christian, willingness to give X days per year, already a donor of record, known for good group skills, etc. Then they identify particular skills, expertise or other characteristics which *some* trustees need to bring for the board to be a good team, e.g., legal expertise, academic experience, fundraising experience, financial acumen, geographical location, gender or racial balance, theological expertise. Finding trustees who have the wisdom, experience, and network, and whose personal lifestyle and spiritual convictions line up with your institution's mission is no small task! The temptation to compromise on a prospective trustee's Christian commitment because of financial status is a very real tension among Christian colleges and universities and must be avoided.

Many boards now have a trustee development committee to organize board profile and keep track of good prospects well in advance of asking them to serve. These potential trustees could be invited to serve on advisory groups, task forces or even board committees as a way of "grooming them" for future board service.

To develop quality boards, it makes sense to give some orientation to nominees *before* they are elected. A practice of "full disclosure" at this point may help a reluctant nominee legitimately say "no" to election. Others will value the opportunity to understand the institution more as part of their preparation for election and their first meeting. Providing copies of the bylaws, standing policies, last audit report, catalog, list of trustees, organization chart, are all helpful pre-election orientation tools, along with a meeting with the board chair and president.

Some aspects of orientation can wait until after elections. These might include a more thorough campus tour, introductions to key administrators, review of recent board and committee minutes, briefing on the budget. Someone on the board needs to be assigned to the orientation program.

Orientation for helping to fulfill advancement goals should be conducted by the chief advancement officer and/or the president. Depending on the campus, this might include a review of the alumni association, development plan, marketing strategies and materials, campus video, and several other "get ready" activities.

With the financial challenges our member institutions face today and in the future, I believe a reasonable goal is to develop a board profile that calls for 80 percent of all new trustees to bring some known capacity for active participation in the advancement goals of the institution. Indeed, I hear more and more people in private colleges saying *all* trustees need to "give, get, or git." In a Christian college or university, however, this is not always the case. There is a very real need for board members who perhaps don't have abundant resources but exceed in their understanding of Scripture, are well networked in the pastoral community, or have academic expertise. The key is to build a well-balanced board!

The Coalition survey asked institutions the question, "What are the main characteristics your board looks for in assessing a new trustee?" Table 7-1 lists their responses in order of importance. To no surprise, spiritual commitment was ranked number one.

Table 7-1
Important Characteristics When Recruiting New Trustees

Involvement	Ranking
Spiritual commitment	1
Leadership (character/reputation)	2
Commitment to mission of college	3
Financial support	4
Professional experience	5
Denominational affiliation	6

While a prospective trustee's spiritual commitment, leadership characteristics, and commitment to the mission of the institution are crucial, they do not by any means detract from the importance of finding those with a genuine willingness to give financially. In fact I cannot think of a situation where a trustee should not be expected to be a donor of record every year. As Christians, we know that God owns everything, has given to us in abundance, expects us to be good stewards of his resources, and expects us to give as it is given to us. This culture of giving grows out of our belief system and provides a good model for others. And it helps the institution's external fundraising. For example, many foundations now ask specifically about the level of giving of trustees. Major donors are encouraged when trustees lead the way. After all, why should anyone else give if trustees themselves are not committed enough to give!

Function 7: Learn the board's governance model.

Learning how to "do governance" well is critical for the board of trustees, both as individuals and collectively. Adopting a paradigm of governance and assuring that new trustees are "up to speed" is a very critical role for any board. Most trustees have served on several nonprofit boards already and bring a whole range of assumptions about how a board works. Unless each board lays out clearly how *it* will govern, there will be continuing frustration, often dysfunction, even chaos during stressful times.

It is impossible for any board or its advancement committee to know nearly enough to "manage" the institution. Yet, to watch many boards is to see groups trying to digest detailed information in order to make management-type decisions. No matter how many committees, reports, and meetings, the task is never-ending. It is impossible to keep up with the information.

Most boards are more reactive than proactive. They wait for the president and cabinet officers to bring items to the board in a "mother may I?" fashion, then try to make a good decision. The problem with this model is that reacting to ad hoc proposals leaves major gaps in a comprehensive set of policies. Another problem is that it tends to signal a "red light" to professionals that says "don't do anything important until you ask the board first." This contributes to a tug-of-war game which tends to inhibit creative and timely decisions on the part of the president. This is dangerous in light of the president's involvement in the fast-paced environment of institutional advancement.

A much better model is the policy governance model made popular by Dr. John Carver in his book **Boards That Make a Difference**. I have modified many of his principles with good effect in working with many boards. Carver would say "give your president the green light" to take decisive action between meetings... but be sure to write good policy parameters in one document first. This document helps the board "speak with one voice" and, again, according to Carver, never needs to exceed a dozen or so pages.

A full standing policies manual would include major sections on mission/results, the governance process itself, board-president/staff relations, and sections on academics, student affairs, finance, and advancement. For this one document—the "one voice" of the board—to work well, normally a key administrator begins the drafting and the appropriate committees focus on writing policies for board approval. In fact, this is the primary work of committees over time—monitoring results and refining policies to move the institution into even more effectiveness.

Function 8: Participate in advancement work.
No matter how good a communicator the president or vice president for advancement is, some public relations activities can be done best by trustees. This is especially true in denominational colleges where church relations are always in need of interpreters and ambassadors of good will.

Trustees individually can open doors for key administrators, talk to friends who may become major donors, interpret the campus to business and political leaders, and help organize alumni. In fact, one reason trustees are recruited is for their networks of friends. Trustees have visibility and credibility in the business, denominational, and other professional communities that are hard to reach by campus personnel. If a trustee has helped the board fulfill its major functions as outlined earlier, there should be a natural desire to "tell the good news" about the campus to friends and acquaintances.

Richard Legon reminds us of a fundamental principle for the 90s: "...if boards target their efforts toward an institution's natural prospects (alumni, parents, institution friends, and area corporations and foundations), there should be sufficient resources available for all" (1989). Trustees, each one doing his or her share, have thousands of these "natural contacts" which can have an enormous impact for good on the advancement efforts at a Christian institution.

Opportunities abound for trustees to help advance their institution. In the admissions area, consider the impact if all trustees simply spoke each year to their church youth group, gave some campus literature to high school juniors, asked the pastor to allow a current student from campus to share during worship, and took time to encourage an interested family. Some trustees can do much more, including opening doors for campus leaders to speak at Rotary, writing a testimony for a publication, or sponsoring a scholarship for an international student. Imagine what would happen if each trustee (recall a board averages 30 people) challenged five young people and their families each year to consider attending their campus.

In public relations, trustees can be of tremendous help. Business leaders, school board and city council members, media personnel, state legislators, and many others need a better understanding of your Christian college. Just remembering that you are a trustee and being willing to share helpful information "on the run" can make a big difference. Lay trustees have tremendous credibility in so many networks that college personnel have difficulty penetrating. Just to open a few doors for the president each year is a tremendous help.

No other group should be as thankful and supportive as college alumni, but they are busy people and often need role models and frequent reminders on how to contribute to building a stronger campus. Alumni who are serving on your board can communicate effectively with this important constituency. Consider ways to involve alumni trustees in reaching the graduate mailing list.

In the area of fundraising, trustees have many expectations placed on them. First, they are expected to support their institution financially. The Coalition survey found that:

- 99 percent of responding trustees contribute to their church
- 68 percent rank their church as the top recipient of their personal giving
- 98 percent contribute to the college where they serve as trustees
- 26 percent ranked the college as the top recipient of their personal support

The survey also asked member institutions to rank their trustees in their ability to give a generous one-time gift (excluding an estate gift). The results are summarized in Table 7-2.

Table 7-2
Trustee Giving Ability

Gift Size	Percentage
Less than $5,000	44%
$5,000 - $25,000	24%
$25,000 - $100,000	18%
More than $100,000	13%

A second fundraising expectation placed on trustees is their responsibility to ask others to give. Many institutions are frustrated that their trustees are not doing more in this area. Unfortunately, what we fail to realize is that many of them, although quite successful in their community, lack the fundamentals in knowing how to help raise support. It is therefore very important that we back up this expectation with sufficient training. James Gregory Lord's book, **The Raising of Money** (1987), and Wesley Willmer's book, **Money for Ministries** (1989), are two good tools to help in this process.

One survey question asked board members to identify what keeps them from actively involving themselves in fundraising. As Table 7-3 shows, a lack of time and training took the top two places.

Table 7-3
Why Trustees Limit Their Involvement in Fundraising

Gift Size	Ranking
Time constraints	1
Lack of fundraising training	2
Not knowing appropriate prospects	3
Reluctance to ask	4
Not asked to help with fundraising	5
Lack of motivation	6
Not the board's responsibility	7

As you can see, there is work to do in this area. In general, I find that trustees feel that their presidents and chief development officers should carry responsibility for fundraising training. Trustees also understand that graduates of Christian colleges generally aspire to service careers that are not well paid, adding to the need for effective development strategies. Fundraising should not be a burden for a trustee, but a privilege. Our Christian colleges and universities should pay careful attention to the interest and needs of each trustee and develop trustee fundraising strategies so each one is comfortable with his or her role and assures maximum, overall effectiveness.

Function 9: Promote advancement committee effectiveness.

Advancement is such a critical area for campus success that almost every board has one or more sub-committees assigned to one or more advancement-related functions. The Coalition survey found that within member institutions:

- 70 percent have an alumni committee

- 70 percent have a public relations committee
- 77 percent have an admissions/recruitment committee
- 88 percent have a fundraising committee

While experts in this area might prefer to have each of these responsibilities assigned to more than one committee, my own preference is to see all four areas under one committee, since they overlap to a considerable degree. Some colleges may, however, assign admissions to a Student Affairs Committee.

Tom Ingram, president of the Association of Governing Boards of Universities and Colleges (AGB), has argued that fundraising should not be delegated to a committee, because it is important for the whole board to be involved (1988). Experience shows, however, that most boards do have an advancement (or "development") committee to help the board fulfill its responsibilities in this area.

The key principle in any board committee work is that committees speak *to* the board, not *for* the board. The full board sets policy. Committees are simply a useful way to manage time and allow some members to specialize on behalf of the board.

My work with many boards has surfaced two general problems. First, committees like to function as "mini boards" setting policies with their vice presidents rather than drawing on vice presidents' knowledge to shape good policy proposals for board action. Second, committees like to make management decisions. Sometimes specific management matters, such as what kind of alumni newsletter works best, are easier and more fun to discuss! Presidents grind their teeth at night thinking about these propensities of their advancement (and other) committees!

In general, committees serve as a group sounding-board for the president and chief advancement officer. This is really a volunteer hat role, but can be part of the committee agenda. The committee should urge staff to seek the best advice possible—from any source—in addition to advice the committee might give. Difficulties arise only when trustees or staff believe committee advice is the same thing as board policy. It is not.

Function 10: Evaluate for maximum advancement effectiveness.

Talented individuals do not automatically function well together as a governing body. The board must provide, often through a trustee development committee, for such things as careful selection of trustees, their orientation and training, by-law review, and evaluation of the board process itself. Any board which focuses on these primary functions and commits to doing them well provides a solid base for institutional advancement which is recognized by those on and off the campus. These are not advisory roles. Board members should view themselves as "owners and stewards," rather than simply volunteers.

The same board development committee that helps in the selection, orientation and training of trustees often is given the assignment of evaluating the board's work. No administrator is in a good position to do this for the board, although you can be sure people outside the board constantly make evaluative judgments about trustees and their decisions!

Evaluation of its president is often a difficult task for a board, but evaluating itself is even more difficult. An annual survey of board members can be useful. Interviews with individual trustees often bring more candid feedback than board discussions about their effectiveness as a group. Inviting an outside facilitator to help the process can be useful. While being sensitive to the feelings of respected colleagues, it is also important to get an honest assessment of how the officers and committee chairs are functioning on behalf of the board. Where problems exist, the majority of most boards will welcome change to become more effective.

One survey question asked institutions to prioritize a list of six indicators used in evaluating trustee effectiveness. Table 7-4 shows the results. It is interesting to note that trustee ability to give money ranked last among Christian colleges and universities. In the institutions outside of the CCCU, it is likely that financial support would rank much closer to the top.

Table 7-4
Ranking of Trustee Effectiveness

Indicators	Ranking
Attendance at board meetings	1
Service on board committees	2
Fundraising	3
Availability to serve the college	4
Wise counsel and expertise	5
Ability to give dollars	6

Trustees also were asked to indicate their level of satisfaction with their own personal involvement in five advancement-related activities on a scale of 1 to 6. For this question, a ranking of "1" indicated a very high level of satisfaction and the number "6" indicated a very low level of satisfaction. The results, shown in Table 7-5, indicate a high level of board involvement in establishing fundraising policy yet with very limited satisfaction in the solicitation of gifts.

Table 7-5
Trustee Satisfaction in Advancement-related Activities

Involvement	Ranking
Deciding fundraising policy	2.5
Making financial contributions	3.4
Assisting admissions efforts	3.7
Referring donor prospects	4.0
Soliciting donors	4.4

One other point regarding evaluation—it is wise for every board to select, instruct, and insist on a debriefing from an external financial audit firm as part of the annual audit. It may be prudent to initiate, as well, periodic legal or program audits to assure board members the institution is in good order.

Regional and specialized accrediting associations give higher education a fairly good method of meeting the tests of external scrutiny. But trustees may want more in-depth, expert opinion on various aspects of campus life within their purview. They should not hesitate to take the initiative, in cooperation with the president, to retain outside expertise when necessary.

Conclusion

Peter Drucker is often quoted as saying an organization must keep asking "who is our customer and what does he value?" College trustees serve as the surrogate market which businesses depend on to plan their futures. Trustees represent the moral owners of a Christian college or university, and their perspectives can be trusted in mapping out the advancement plans that will enhance campus goals.

Yes, successful college advancement begins with a board of trustees which understands and fulfills its governing role, plus expects its individual members to contribute to the work of admissions, public relations, alumni relations, and fund-raising. To enjoy such a board requires hard work from the president and a desire on the part of the board itself to learn and apply good board principles.

Christian colleges and universities compete in a relatively stable-state sector of more than 3,400 institutions, all becoming more sophisticated in advancement functions. Most of these other campuses have either state government support or larger endowments. People are attracted to values-oriented campuses once they know about them. Advancement—incoming good advancement board policies—is the key variable in whether a college thrives or just survives.

Our survey research showed trustees themselves recognize they are not doing as well as they should in the area of advancement/development. This is the time to use the good materials available for improving trustee selection, orientation, training, evaluation, and volunteer leadership. It is also the time to remember that our work is the Lord's work and allow him to light our paths and guide our steps. Without Christ at the center of the education we offer, our mission is hollow and our work will be in vain.

RESOURCES

Breneman, David W. **Liberal Arts Colleges: Thriving, Surviving or Endangered?** Washington, DC: The Brookings Institution, 1994.

Carver, John. **Boards That Make a Difference**. San Francisco, CA: Jossey-Bass Publishers, 1990.

Chait, Richard P., Holland, Thomas, and Taylor, Barbara. **The Effective Board of Trustees.** Washington, DC: Oryz Press, American Council on Education, 1993.

Clugston, R. Wayne. "Advancing Through the Looking Glass: A Servant Leadership Perspective for the Small College" in **Advancing the Small College: New Directions for Institutional Advancement.** No. 13. Edited by Wesley K. Willmer. San Francisco: Jossey-Bass Inc., 1981.

Cowan, Ruth B. **A Prescription for Vitality for Small, Private Colleges**. Washington, DC: Association of Governing Boards, 1994.

Gale, Robert. "The Role of Governing the Board," in **The President and Fund Raising**, ed. by James L. Fisher and Gary H. Quehl. New York: Macmillan, 1989, 102.

Growther, Connie. "Building a Better Board," **Currents.** November/December 1989, 22f.

Herman, Robert D. and Heimovics, Richard D. **Executive Leadership in Nonprofit Organizations**. San Francisco, CA: Jossey-Bass Publishers, 1991.

Hobbs, Walter C. "Positioning a Small College" in **Advancing the Small College: New Directions for Institutional Advancement.** No. 13. Edited by Wesley K. Willmer. San Francisco: Jossey-Bass, Inc., 1981.

Howe, Fisher. **Fund Raising and the Nonprofit Board Member**. Washington, DC: National Center for Nonprofit Boards, 1988.

Howe, Fisher. **The Board Member's Guide to Fund Raising**. San Francisco, CA: Jossey-Bass Publishers, 1991.

Hurtubise, Mark and Bishop, Laurence A. "Who are 'Successful' Fund-Raising Presidents?" **AGB Reports**, March/April 1991, 33.

Legon, Richard D. **The Fund-Raising Role.** Washington, DC. AGB Pocket Guide, No. 6, 1989.

Lord, James Gregory. **The Raising of Money: Thirty-Five Essentials Every Trustee Should Know.** Cleveland, OH: Third Sector Press, 1990.

Nason, J. W. **The Nature of Trusteeship: The Role and Responsibilities of College and University Boards**. Washington, DC: The Association of Governing Boards of Universities and Colleges, 1982.

Neff, Charles B. and Leondar, Barbara. **Presidential Search: A Guide to the Process of Selecting and Appointing College and University Presidents**. Washington, DC: Association of Governing Boards, 1992.

Neff, Robert W. "The Trustees' Critical Role in Small College Advancement" in **Winning Strategies in Challenging Times for Advancing Small Colleges.** Edited by Wesley K. Willmer. Washington, DC: Council for the Advancement and Support of Education, 1993.

Pocock, J. W. **Fund Raising Leadership.** Washington, DC: The Association of Governing Boards, 1989.

The best information on college and other nonprofit boards is shown below:

1. Association of Governing Boards of Universities and Colleges, Washington, DC. Request their most recent Trustee Resource Guide. Phone: 202/296-8400. Fax: 202/223-7053.

2. National Center for Nonprofit Boards, Washington, DC. Request their most recent catalog of resources. Phone: 202/452-6262. Fax: 202/452-6299.

About the Author

ROBERT C. ANDRINGA became the fourth president of the Coalition for Christian Colleges & Universities July 1, 1994. During the prior nine years he consulted with chief executives and their boards in the nonprofit sector. Earlier assignments included Republican staff director of the Education and Labor Committee of the U.S. House of Representatives; director of policy research for the governor of Minnesota, and executive director of the Education Commission of the States. He has trained more than 1,000 trustees in their roles at colleges, church and parachurch agencies, and other nonprofit organizations.

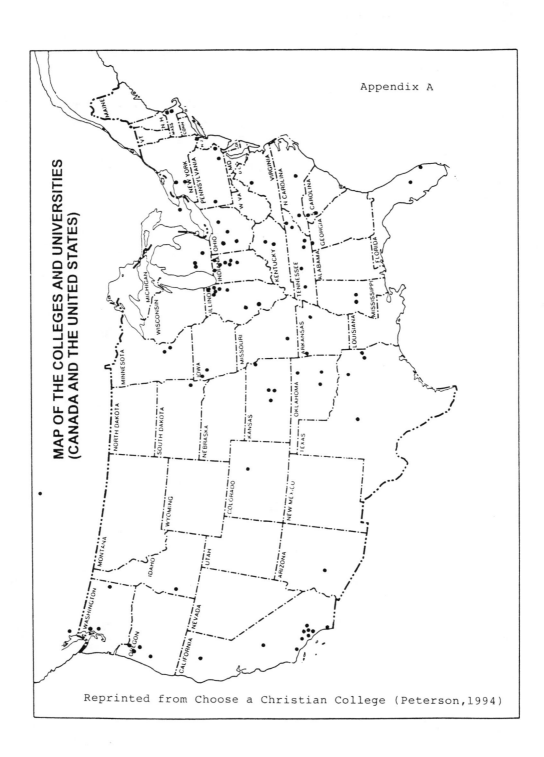

Appendix A

MAP OF THE COLLEGES AND UNIVERSITIES
(CANADA AND THE UNITED STATES)

Reprinted from Choose a Christian College (Peterson,1994)

CHRISTIAN COLLEGE COALITION
LILLY PROJECT FOR FUND RAISING EFFECTIVENESS

RESOURCE DEVELOPMENT SURVEY

As one means of assessing the value of the Christian College Coalition's Lilly Project for Fund Raising Effectiveness to the member colleges, we wish to repeat the 1989 survey of institutional development/ advancement office operations. As you will note, this questionnaire seeks descriptive data about your programs in fund raising, alumni affairs, and public relations, along with an analysis of trustee board involvement in these activities. Also, included at the end of the survey are several questions specifically about the Lilly Project.

If any answer is not readily obtainable, please use an average or educated estimation. Thank you in advance for your careful and prompt attention to this survey.

Name of Institution_____

Name of Respondent _____

Respondent's Title _____ Phone (_____) _____

1. Check the number of (FTE) undergraduate students (fall, 1993).

    (1) _____up to 500   (5) _____1251-1500
    (2) _____501-750   (6) _____1501-2000
    (3) _____751-1000   (7) _____2001 and over
    (4) _____1001-1250

2. If the institution offers graduate programs, what was the fall 1993 enrollment? _____FTE

3. How long has the institution been in existence?

    (1) _____less than 10 years   (4) _____51 to 75 years
    (2) _____11 to 25 years   (5) _____76 to 100 years
    (3) _____26 to 50 years   (6) _____more than 100 years

4. If the institution is affiliated with a denomination, which one? _____

5. Check the professional organizations to which the institution belongs. AGB_____ CASE_____
    ECFA_____ CSA_____ CMMA_____ NSFRE_____

6. What is the total FY 1992-93 educational and general (E&G) expenditure, including student aid, for the institution? $ _____

7. What is the size of the institution's endowment? $ _____

8. What percentage of the educational budget is met by the following?

    tuition   _____%
    gift income   _____%
    income from endowment   _____%
    other   _____% Specify_____
                    TOTAL   100   %

GOVERNING BOARD OF TRUSTEES

9. How many voting members are there on the board? Total: _____

    Of these, how many are women? _____ How many are persons of color? _____

10. Do you feel the trustees are adequately trained in fund raising? _____ yes _____ no

11. If yours is a church-related institution, what percentage of the board must be members of the founding denomination? _____%

    What percentage of the board is appointed through the denomination? _____%

12. What professional occupations are represented on the board?

clergy	_____%	lawyers	_____%	
business	_____%	doctors	_____%	
educators	_____%	other	_____%	Specify_____

13. What percentage of the board is capable of making a one-time gift (excluding an estate gift) of:

not more than $5,000	_____%
>$5,000 but not more than $25,000	_____%
>$25,000 but not more than $100,000	_____%
more than $100,000	_____%
TOTAL	100 %

14. Is there an active, working board committee responsible for (one committee could handle all):

admissions/recruitment	_____ yes _____ no	fund raising	_____ yes _____ no
alumni affairs	_____ yes _____ no	public relations	_____ yes _____ no

15. What percentage of the trustees are alumni? _____%

16. To what extent are you satisfied with the trustees' involvement in the following areas? (Please fill in the number that indicates most closely the level of your satisfaction--"1" is you are very satisfied, ranging to "6" if you are very dissatisfied.)

    _____ deciding fund raising policy   _____ soliciting donors
    _____ making financial contributions   _____ assisting admissions efforts
    _____ referring donor prospects

STAFFING AND BUDGET

17. In which of these functions do volunteers (other than trustees) play an active role?

admissions/recruitment	_____ yes _____ no	fund raising	_____ yes _____ no
alumni affairs	_____ yes _____ no	public relations	_____ yes _____ no

18. Please list the total paid staff (FTE) for these functions: (If a person shares responsibilities, show % in appropriate locations.)

	Professional	Clerical/Secretarial
admissions/recruitment	_____ FTE	_____ FTE
alumni affairs	_____ FTE	_____ FTE
fund raising	_____ FTE	_____ FTE
public relations	_____ FTE	_____ FTE
TOTAL	_____ FTE	_____ FTE

19. Of the total fund raising FTE "professional" category, how is this time divided among these four areas?

annual giving _____ FTE	prospect research _____ FTE
capital giving _____ FTE	planned giving _____ FTE
(include foundations here)	

20. Are there plans to enlarge this staff in the next two years? _____ yes _____ no _____ don't know

If yes, how many new people will be added? _____ professional FTE _____ clerical FTE

21. Has there been an increase in the staff in the last four years? _____ yes _____ no

If yes, by how many? _____ FTE

22. Please rate the following activities among constituents according to their helpfulness in raising funds. (1=extremely helpful to 6=no help)

	suggest prospects	visit/call prospects	rate prospects	provide advice
trustees	_____ /	_____ /	_____ /	_____
alumni	_____ /	_____ /	_____ /	_____
parents	_____ /	_____ /	_____ /	_____
friends	_____ /	_____ /	_____ /	_____
faculty/staff	_____ /	_____ /	_____ /	_____

23. In FY 1992-93, what were the total institutional expenditures (including salaries and benefits, travel, media-promotion, etc.) to perform these functions:

admissions/recruitment $ _____	fund raising $ _____
alumni affairs $ _____	public relations $ _____
	TOTAL EXPENDITURES $ _____

24. Have professional consultants been used in the management of any of these four functions in the last year? If yes, indicate number of days per month.

admissions/recruitment	_____ yes _____ no _____ number of days per month
alumni affairs	_____ yes _____ no _____ number of days per month
fund raising	_____ yes _____ no _____ number of days per month
public relations	_____ yes _____ no _____ number of days per month

25. What keeps the institution from using consultants more? _____

26. Please rate the emphasis you place on each of the following fund-raising activities. (1=high emphasis, 6= no emphasis)

_____alumni class reunion gifts   _____direct mail
_____separate parents' fund   _____personal solicitation
_____gift clubs   _____foundations
_____premiums by phone and/or mail   _____other
_____fund-raising banquets

ALUMNI

27. How many off-campus alumni meetings are conducted annually? _____

28. Is fund raising a responsibility of the alumni association? _____yes _____no

29. If you answered "yes" to question 30, is there general satisfaction with how the alumni association fulfills this responsibility? _____yes _____no

30. Is there a special alumni program for recent graduates? _____yes _____no

31. What percentage of total gift support came from alumni in FY 1992-93? _____%

32. What percentage of alumni made a gift during FY 1992-93? _____%

FUND RAISING

33. What percentage of total gift support in FY 1992-93 was for annual unrestricted monies? _____%

34. Has the institution conducted a capital campaign in the last three years? _____yes _____no

35. Are there plans to conduct a capital campaign in the next three years? _____yes _____no

36. Indicate the total gift support received in FY 1992-93:

     capital $_____   operations $_____   endowment $_____

37. Think about the 50 largest donors to the institution. Of these people, what percentage of the face-to-face calls to ask for funds are made by:

_____% trustees   _____% volunteers
_____% president   _____% other   Specify_____
_____% staff   TOTAL   100 %

38. Please rank these fund raising activities according to the amount of gift income generated. (1 indicates the most income, 2 indicates the second largest amount of income, etc.) Leave blank those activities not used by the institution.

_____direct mail   _____area representatives
_____telemarketing (phonathons)   _____personal contact
_____radio programs/spots   _____special events (banquets, etc.)
_____TV programs/spots   _____other   Specify_____
_____church relations

39. Please indicate what percentage of total gift income is given by sources below. (Leave blank if item does not apply.)

_____% alumni	_____% foundations
_____% parents	_____% businesses
_____% trustees	_____% churches
_____% faculty	_____% deferred gifts (wills, bequests)
_____% individuals	_____% government grants
_____% students (not tuition)	_____% other Specify_____

TOTAL   100 %

40. Is the institution currently involved in a campaign to increase endowment?   _____yes _____no

41. In the last five years, has a market analysis (who gives and why) of the institution's donor constituency been conducted?   _____yes _____no

42. What is the size of the fund-raising mailing list?   alumni   _____
others   _____
TOTAL   _____

43. What was the total percentage of those on the mailing list who gave at least one gift in FY 1992-93?

_____0-10%   _____11-20%   _____21-35%   _____36-50%   _____51-75%   _____above 75%
_____not sure

44. How many times were the following sent in FY 1992-93 to the clientele of the institution? (Leave blank any category which does not apply.)

_____newsletters/magazines	_____to lapsed donors
_____general appeal letters for funds	_____to non-donors
_____segmented appeals:	_____to follow up first-time donors
_____to major donors	_____other Specify_____
_____to regular donors	

INSTITUTIONAL FOUNDATION

45. Does the institution have a legally separate foundation for the purpose of raising funds?   _____yes _____no

   a. If YES, when was the foundation established? _____

   b. If NO, is there consideration of establishing such a foundation?   _____yes _____no

46. What is the relationship between the boards of the institution and the foundation? _____

_____

_____

47. Does the foundation have a paid director?   _____yes _____no

   a. If YES, is the director employed full-time?   _____yes _____no

   b. If the director is not employed full-time, what percentage of full-time is s/he employed? _____%

c. What is the annual base salary? $_____

48. Does the foundation maintain an office on the campus? _____yes _____no

    a. If NO, where is the foundation office located? _____

    _____

    _____

    b. If YES, does the institution provide basic services to the foundation (e.g. utilities, housekeeping, maintenance, support staff)? _____yes _____no

    c. If YES to 48b, is there a charge to the foundation for such services? _____yes _____no

49. Are foundation employees paid through the institutional payroll? _____yes _____no

50. Do foundation employees have the same fringe benefits as do equivalent college employees?
    _____yes _____no

    If NO, what are the primary differences? _____

    _____

    _____

PUBLIC RELATIONS

51. "I think the image of the institution should be modified to more adequately satisfy the needs of our clientele." (Please mark the appropriate section on the scale.)

    Strongly agree_____/_____/_____/_____/_____/_____Strongly disagree

52. Modification of the organization's image is primarily the responsibility of the: (Check one.)

    _____board _____president _____advancement office _____other Specify_____

53. Using the indicated code, specify the importance of the following public relations goals for the institution: (For each goal, indicate 1 if of great importance, ranging to 6 if of little importance.)

    _____attract prospective students   _____enhance favorable relations with the faculty
    _____add to the college's academic reputation _____promote favorable relations with the community
    _____report news   _____educate the public about higher education
    _____raise funds   _____show the importance of religion in education
    _____provide a community service   _____build and hold goodwill for the institution

54. Does the institution have a public relations advisory group comprised of people outside the institution (other than trustees)? _____yes _____no

55. Has the institution conducted a readership survey of its primary publication in the past three years?
    _____yes _____no

56. Is the public relations office responsible for student recruitment literature? _____yes _____no

57. What kind of image is the institution trying to convey? Rank these image elements from 1 to 8, 1 being the most important, 8 the least.

_____quality academics	_____Christian character
_____fiscal stability	_____research activity
_____service to community	_____service to church
_____teaching quality	_____"Christian" occupations of alumni

58. Is there a written, budgeted plan to improve the institution's image in the community? _____yes _____no

LILLY PROJECT FOR FUND RAISING EFFECTIVENESS

As the Coalition's Lilly-funded Project for Fund Raising Effectiveness draws to a close, it is important that we be able to report to the Endowment what this initiative has accomplished on behalf of the membership. Your candid response to the following questions will constitute one avenue for assessment of the programs and services provided to member colleges during the past three years.

59. The following list of statements is drawn from the goals listed in the Coalition's proposal to the Endowment. Based on what you and/or others at your institution have experienced of the grant programs, please respond to each of the statements by placing an "x" in the appropriate column.

	Strongly agree	Agree	Disagree	Strongly disagree	No opinion
a. The selection of workshop topics reflects an understanding of the fund-raising challenges which member institutions face.	_____	/_____	/_____	/_____	/_____
b. Lilly Project activities are well-organized.	_____	/_____	/_____	/_____	/_____
c. Registration fees or other charges for Lilly Project activities have encouraged participation by member institutions.	_____	/_____	/_____	/_____	/_____
d. The centralized leadership of the Project has contributed to its usefulness for the institution.	_____	/_____	/_____	/_____	/_____
e. The Lilly Project has helped foster information networks among development staff of member institutions.	_____	/_____	/_____	/_____	/_____
f. The Lilly Project has encouraged discussion of the spiritual dimension of fund raising.	_____	/_____	/_____	/_____	/_____
g. The Lilly Project has assisted presidents and trustees in their understanding of the distinctives of serving on the board of a Christian college or university.	_____	/_____	/_____	/_____	/_____
h. The Lilly Project has raised the "comfort level" of presidents with their roles in fund raising.	_____	/_____	/_____	/_____	/_____

	Strongly agree	Agree	Disagree	Strongly disagree	No opinion
i. The Lilly Project has addressed the need to attract greater numbers of major donors to the institutions.	_____/	_____/	_____/	_____/	_____
j. Lilly Project activities have encouraged team building and synergism of effort between presidents, trustees, and development personnel.	_____/	_____/	_____/	_____/	_____
k. The Lilly Project has served to highlight fund raising success stories among the member institutions.	_____/	_____/	_____/	_____/	_____
l. The Lilly Project has helped link Christian College Coalition activities with those of other fund-raising training organizations such as CASE, AGB, NSFRE, and CSA.	_____/	_____/	_____/	_____/	_____

60. What activities from the Lilly Project would you most like to see continued by the Christian College Coalition? (Please rank order.)

_____*DevelopLink* newsletter
_____Pre-annual meeting workshops for presidents
_____Annual gathering of CDOs
_____Development office audits
_____Summer retreat for presidential couples
_____CCC dinner at CSA annual meeting
_____Campus-based trustee education services
_____Resident fund-raising "expert" on CCC national staff
_____Special topic workshops (e.g. annual fund, campaigning, planned giving, proposal writing, etc.)
_____Other   Specify_____

61. What message would you like to send to the Lilly Endowment as evaluation of their investment in the fund-raising effectiveness of member institutions? _____

_____

_____

Thank you for your time and cooperation. Please use the enclosed envelope to return this questionnaire by April 15 to:

Christian College Coalition
c/o Jane Halteman
515 E. Prairie
Wheaton, IL 60187

Responding Institutions

Asbury College
Wilmore, KY

Azusa Pacific University
Azusa, CA

Bartlesville Wesleyan College
Bartlesville, OK

Belhaven College
Jackson, MS

Bethel College
Mishawaka, IN

Bethel College
North Newton, KS

Bethel College
St. Paul, MN

Biola University
La Mirada, CA

Bluffton College
Bluffton, OH

Bryan College
Dayton, TN

California Baptist College
Riverside, CA

Calvin College
Grand Rapids, MI

Campbell University
Buies Creek, NC

Campbellsville College
Campbellsville, KY

Colorado Christian University
Lakewood, CO

Cornerstone College
Grand Rapids, MI

Covenant College
Lookout Mountain, GA

Dallas Baptist University
Dallas, TX

Dordt College
Sioux Center, IA

Eastern College
St. Davids, PA

Eastern Mennonite University
Harrisonburg, VA

Eastern Nazarene College
Quincy, MA

Erskine College
Due West, SC

Evangel College
Springfield, MO

Fresno Pacific College
Fresno, CA

Geneva College
Beaver Falls, PA

George Fox College
Newberg, OR

Gordon College
Wenham, MA

Goshen College
Goshen, IN

Grace College
Winona Lake, IN

Greenville College
Greenville, IL

Houghton College
Houghton, NY

Huntington College
Huntington, IN

Indiana Wesleyan University
Marion, IN

John Brown University
Siloam Springs, AR

Judson College
Elgin, IL

King College
Bristol, TN

The King's College
Briarcliff Manor, NY

The King's University College
Edmonton, AB

LeTourneau University
Longview, TX

Malone College
Canton, OH

Messiah College
Grantham, PA

MidAmerica Nazarene College
Olathe, KS

Milligan College
Milligan College, TN

Montreat College
Montreat, NC

Mount Vernon Nazarene College
Mount Vernon, OH

North Park College
Chicago, IL

Northwest College
Kirkland, WA

Northwest Christian College
Eugene, OR

Northwest Nazarene College
Nampa, ID

Northwestern College
Orange City, IA

Northwestern College
Roseville, MN

Palm Beach Atlantic College
West Palm Beach, FL

Point Loma Nazarene College
San Diego, CA

Redeemer College
Ancaster, ON

Roberts Wesleyan College
Rochester, NY

Seattle Pacific University
Seattle, WA

Simpson College
Redding, CA

Southern California College
Costa Mesa, CA

Southern Nazarene University
Bethany, OK

Southern Wesleyan University
Central, SC

Spring Arbor College
Spring Arbor, MI

Sterling College
Sterling, KS

Tabor College
Hillsboro, KS

Taylor University
Upland, IN

Trevecca Nazarene College
Nashville, TN

Trinity Christian College
Palos Heights, IL

Trinity Western University
Langley, BC

Union University
Jackson, TN

University of Sioux Falls
Sioux Falls, SD

Warner Pacific College
Portland, OR

Western Baptist College
Salem, OR

Westmont College
Santa Barbara, CA

Wheaton College
Wheaton, IL

Whitworth College
Spokane, WA

About the Author-Editor

WESLEY K. WILLMER has been involved in Christian higher education for almost 30 years, first as a student and then in professional administrative and teaching roles at Wheaton College, Roberts Wesleyan College, and Seattle Pacific University. He is vice president of university advancement at Biola University in La Mirada, California, where he is responsible for enrollment management, alumni, university relations, marketing, development, and intercollegiate athletics.

*This is his seventh book in the college advancement field. His most recent book, **Winning Strategies in Challenging Times for Advancing Small Colleges**, was published in 1993 by the Council for Advancement and Support of Education (CASE) and received the 1995 Staley/Robeson/Ryan/St. Lawrence Research Prize honorable mention for significant contribution to the body of knowledge in philanthropy and fundraising from the National Society of Fund Raising Executives (NSFRE). He edited two books published by the Christian College Coalition—in 1990 **Friends, Funds, and Freshmen: A Manager's Guide to Christian College Advancement** and in 1987 **Friends, Funds, and Freshmen for Christian Colleges: A Manager's Guide to Advancing Resource Development**. He was the guest editor of **Advancing the Small College**, published by Jossey-Bass in 1982 as part of the "New Directions for Institutional Advancement" series and two books previously published by CASE—**The Small College Advancement Program: Managing for Results** in 1981 and **A New Look at Managing the Small College Advancement Program** in 1987. Willmer also has contributed many articles for magazines and professional journal publications.*

In 1986 CASE selected Willmer from among its 14,000 members to receive its annual Alice Beeman award for significant contributions in research and writing, and he currently serves on the CASE Commission on Philanthropy.

*As a result of chairing the 1987 national conference, "Funding the Christian Challenge," Willmer also edited **Money for Ministries** in 1989. He serves as chair of the board of the Christian Stewardship Association. In the last few years, he has initiated and obtained grants of more than $1 million to study and improve nonprofit management practices. He also serves on the board of administration for the National Association of Evangelicals.*

*He holds a B.A. in psychology and M.Ed. in counseling and guidance from Seattle Pacific University. He earned a Ph.D. in higher education from the State University of New York at Buffalo under the advisorship of A. Westley Rowland, editor-in-chief of the **Handbook of Institutional Advancement**. Willmer resides in Fullerton, California, with his wife, Sharon, and three children—Brian, Kristell, and Stephen.*